One Surgeon's Soft War

Bernard Williams

Library of Congress Control Number: 2016904415
ISBN: Hardcover   978-1-5144-7601-7
                   Softcover   978-1-5144-7602-4
                   eBook   978-1-5144-7600-0

Print information available on the last page.

Rev. date: 6 May 2016

To order additional copies of this book, contact:
Xlibris
1-888-795-4274
www.Xlibris.com
Orders@Xlibris.com
533424

List of Illustrations

To Rosalind
With grateful thanks to a Providence which
smiled on me so often while scowling
on so many others

Contents

Foreword

Bernard Williams was born in Swansea on 26th August 1910, the elder son of Morgan and Beryl Williams. The family was strongly medical—Dr Morgan Williams was a GP in Morriston and Beryl's brother Howell Gabe was a surgeon at Swansea General Hospital. Bernard was educated at Marlborough College, Gonville and Caius College, Cambridge, and St Thomas' Hospital, London, qualifying in medicine in 1932. He trained as a surgeon and, anticipating the outbreak of war, joined the Royal Army Medical Corps in 1939. *One Surgeon's Soft War* is a highly personal account of his experiences in Europe and North Africa, where he was at El Alamein and dealt with many casualties.

He met Rosalind in Cairo, and they were married in 1943. After the war they settled in Portsmouth, where Bernard practised general surgery until his retirement in 1975 when they moved to Hayling Island. Bernard was blessed with a formidable memory, as manifested by this book. He was always a great communicator: as the family grew up he kept everyone regularly updated with all the family news via a typed carbon-copied newsletter. This was originally named the Helena Times, after the family home in Helena Road, Southsea, and subsequently renamed the Maytree Mail after the house in Hayling Island.

Bernard died in 2001 at the age of 91, and Rosalind died four years later at the age of 93. This book not only chronicles his wartime experiences but also gives much insight into his personality. It is full of self-deprecating wit and humorous anecdote, as well as insights into the futility of war, and the frailty of leaders. We hope it will be of interest to the layman, military historians and members of the medical profession, and indeed to anyone who values a look behind the scenes at both the tragedy and the humour to be found in life generally.

As a tribute to their long partnership, both Bernard and Rosalind have their names inscribed together on the Wall of Honour at the Royal Society of Medicine.

Tim, John and Peter Williams, and Jane Shaw.
April 2016

Preface

Of course war can never be described as "soft"; but the Second World War was to me personally remarkably kind, when I think of what befell so many of my compatriots. I had joined a few months before the declaration of war in 1939 one of the Army Reserves, which was entitled the 'Supplementary Reserve Category C'. It was intended to be a reserve of specialists, which was a somewhat flattering title that took no account of experience. To join, all one needed was a higher degree, and I had become a Fellow of the Royal College of Surgeons of England in 1937. The War Office was anxious that summer to have a theoretical staff in post. Clearly, in the event of war the place of a young man was to be in the forces, so when I saw the advertisement it seemed too good a chance to miss. It proved one of the best things I ever did. For the six years the conflict lasted, I was never without a good and interesting job. For five and a half of them I served in 'operational areas' abroad, my total home service amounting to less than a year. I spent much of the time in Base Hospitals, but the three stints of forward area work that I did were in advances, not retreats. War is one thing when one is winning, and very much another when one is going backwards.

I hardly ever went hungry, and never thirsty, thanks to the splendid supply services. With a LiLo inflatable mattress that never gave out, a camp bed and sleeping bag, and a folding chair, discomfort was rare. I even acquired a taste for sleeping under canvas, which I continued to indulge in family holidays after the war and still enjoy.

I was much blessed too in the matter of health, which remained good throughout apart from sandfly fever, 'Gyppie Tummy', a carbuncle on my bottom in the Middle East, and dysentery in Germany. Injuries were confined to a temporary loss of sight in one eye caused by a hyphaema (blood in the anterior chamber of the eye) due to a tennis ball, and a black eye from a champagne cork in the course of celebrating VE Day.

My total Army service lasted nearly seven years. It must be unique in one respect, in that I never attended a formal parade, involving drill and marching. In the frenzy of the early days when we were being kitted out, and a little later setting up and running a 1,200 bedded hospital in France, there was no time for such military niceties. The same held good for four years in the Middle East, and the final advance through Germany. At the time of the German surrender to Montgomery at Luneberg, my little Field Surgical Unit, stationed nearby, was ordered to take part in the Victory Parade a short time later. There followed some mad spitting and polishing, and indeed some practice drilling and marching, after which I felt we wouldn't disgrace ourselves too much. Alas, Fate denied us this chance to display our newfound skills, as, when the great day dawned, it was drenching with rain, which continued for many hours. The parade was called off.

Reginald Murley (later to become President of the Royal College of Surgeons of England) was also in the neighbourhood at the time, and records his recollections in his delightful biography *Surgical Roots and Branches*. He was a Territorial and had been in the Army from the beginning. He aptly describes his Army years as being spent in the 'Great University of Life'. How right he was!

I feel a lasting gratitude towards, and affection for, the RAMC (Royal Army Medical Corps), in which it was an honour to serve. The motto of the Corps is 'In Arduis Fidelis', which has been freely translated as 'Faithful under peculiarly difficult circumstances'. Sometimes, indeed, but by no means always!

The numerous letters I wrote home to my parents in the early years have helped in the compilation of this little book. I have also drawn freely on my wife's recollections. She has been blessed with a very good memory. I wrote too to Lady Chiesman, known as 'Darloo', and a friend of many years standing who also kept the letters and returned them to me not long ago. On active service, it was a court martial offence to keep a diary, so I stuck to this rule, as it seemed reasonable security-wise. How far the many highly placed officers who made fortunes by publishing their experiences after the war adhered to the rules in this respect I would not know, but I suspect that many of them did not.

Another helpful thing has been my perhaps curious addiction to typing. This started well before the war, and I was rarely without my portable typewriter, which I cherished and guarded throughout the conflict. If I can lay claim to any fame in the RAMC, it was because I always typed my operation notes in red, no doubt an appropriate colour!

Latterly, in retirement, encouraged by our two elder sons, I have taken up word processing. The first machine I learned to use was an Amstrad, and from that, I graduated to a more modern IBM-compatible make, a Winstation, which was subsequently exchanged for an IBM Aptiva, thanks to the good offices of my IBM friend, John Perry. This last model is very fast and a considerable improvement on its predecessor. I never cease to marvel at what it can do, which often outstrips my capacity to comprehend or to use it's full potential. In conclusion, I would like to express my gratitude to Mrs Diana Giffard and Miss Audrey White whose skill with word processors and other modern devices have made the production of this little book possible.

Bernard Williams
Hayling Island, 1995

Postscript, April 2016: This book was originally published in small numbers in 1996. The family is grateful to John and Sherry Tippey for facilitating this reprint, in which some additional images have been included.

Chapter 1

The Early Days

In 1939 the activities of Herr Hitler, who had fought as a corporal in World War One, and later for political reasons changed his name from that of Schicklgruber, were causing increasing alarm. He was not very fond of the British, who had gassed him in the trenches. In 1938, he had been responsible for the Anschluss with Austria, his homeland, and duped Mr Neville Chamberlain, the then Prime Minister, in Munich. Mr Chamberlain, an essentially decent man, had flown back in triumph therefrom in September 1938. On emerging from the aeroplane, he waved a piece of paper and quoted 'From this nettle danger, we have snatched this flower, safety'. Hitler's aims, he said, were peaceable. Few of us believed that Herr Adolf would go to the lengths of starting another world war while the memories of the horrors of the last one were still fresh in the minds of so many. In addition, gruesome reports of the happenings of the Spanish Civil War had been filling the newspapers daily for more than two years. Anti-war feeling ran high. We did not then know that the German Ambassador, Ribbentrop, an ex-champagne salesman, had informed his boss that Britain was unlikely to fight, a belief fortified by a debate held in the Oxford Union in 1933 entitled 'This House will under no circumstances fight for King and Country.' A comfortable majority carried the motion. Little did those rather cynical young men know what they were doing, or that soon they were to be put to the test.

The Armed Services were busy building up their reserves. I, along with several of my friends, felt that, if there had to be a war, the services would be the place to be. The question before us was which one to choose. One friend plumped for the RAF as he felt it offered the best chance of a bath in fresh water for the duration of any possible conflict, while another chose the RN because it provided a stand for the Times at breakfast and maintained a tradition of no talking at that meal. I had been fascinated by stories told by an uncle who had been a surgeon in Casualty Clearing Stations in France in World War One and whose work had gained him an OBE. In his case at least, I felt that those initials did not stand for 'Other Buggers' Efforts'. I decided too that the Army would provide the most valuable experience as far as I was concerned, especially when it invented its reserve of 'specialists' who required little more than a higher degree to be eligible. The choice of service was not therefore a difficult one for me. This was an opportunity not to be missed. I had become a Fellow of the Royal College of Surgeons in 1937, following a stroke of luck in the finals. I had managed to cut my finger in operating on a corpse, into the abdomen of which I had bled profusely. The examiner said, 'I see you are having difficulty with the haemostasis'. He went back to his table delighted with his quip. I saw him and his colleague rolling about with laughter as I approached, and in excellent humour. Thereafter I could do no wrong. My further training went smoothly, and in 1939 I found myself working as a Registrar at my Alma Mater, St Thomas' Hospital, complete with an English Fellowship.

I wrote to the War Office and was duly instructed to report to Whitehall, which was within easy walking distance. So off I went and found myself in that then remarkably silent mausoleum. From a notice board there fluttered a yellowing piece of paper announcing a dance held the best part of a year before. At last I found someone who told me that I was in the wrong building and directed me to a small office in one of those little towers that flanked the entrance to Horse Guards Parade across the road. There, I was greeted by a magnificent officer, monocled and shod in shining field boots. He proffered a Turkish cigarette, then very much de rigeur, with the words 'Have a gasper, old chap.' I did not smoke but deemed it prudent to accept. He then waxed eloquent about the delights of service in the regular army, while I admired his boots, which were on the desk in front of him. Reluctantly I confessed that I only wanted to join in the event of war. In that case, he told me, I would have to produce my Fellowship Diploma at Millbank, and duly made an appointment. There a friendly major unrolled the document and scanned it thoughtfully. 'This is a damn fine diploma, but I'm afraid I have no idea what to do with it' was his comment. I forbore tactfully from making any suggestions, and to my relief he handed it back. Two weeks later, I had a letter informing me that I was in. In the event of the Reserve being called up I was to report at once to Netley near Southampton as Junior Surgical Specialist to No 3 General Hospital, which was being mobilised there. My rank was that of Lieutenant. My pay as a reservist was £20 a year, which I found a welcome addition to my annual salary of £220 as a Registrar. I was obliged to attend camp once a year, but as it happened, there was no opportunity to fulfil that duty before the Reserve was called up. So on 1 September 1939 I found myself in Waterloo Station with a group of other bewildered people, boarding a train bound for Netley. Included among them was my good old friend Bob Nevin, with whom I had worked in St Thomas', where he was the Resident Assistant Surgeon (the senior resident), when I was a House Surgeon. He was a most loyal and efficient chap, and the soul of integrity. He was later to become Clinical Dean of the Medical School at St Thomas', and a famous one at that. Under his aegis, the school enjoyed a Golden Era. The main Lecture Theatre is named after him in grateful commemoration. On this occasion, he was on his way to take up the post of surgeon to a Casualty Clearing Station.

Chapter 2

Netley

Netley Hospital on the Solent was a huge barracks of a place which rumour had it had been designed for Hong Kong. There we were kitted out with uniforms and gas masks, which we were required to try out in a chamber filled with tear gas. This proved almost fatal for Colonel Foster, a plethoric and irascible man, who emerged coughing and spluttering, and a rich shade of puce. 'I couldn't get any bloody air at all' was his comment, the statement confirmed by his cyanotic appearance. On 3 September, we listened to Neville Chamberlain's fateful broadcast with foreboding.

After a few days we were informed that our tented hospital with all its equipment was on its way and due to arrive at Netley Station at 3 a.m. A small posse of us was detailed to meet it. The train arrived at 8 a.m. It comprised a long string of trucks, each covered by tarpaulins. On uncovering the first truck, we found it full of boots, as indeed were all the others. It transpired that our hospital had gone to Aldershot while we had received the army's reserve of footwear instead. There had been an unfortunate mistake.

In charge of the surgical division at this time was an ebullient character from Llanelli, where he had been a GP. He had served in the First World War and arrived wearing an 'Old Bill' or 'Gor Blimey' type of hat, i.e. a military cap from which the stiffener had been removed, which he wore at a jaunty angle. Lt. Col. Smith was a small man with pronounced views on most things, which he tended to deliver at the top of his voice. He never stopped talking, or indeed smoking cigarettes. Soon known as 'Chattering Charlie', he rapidly incurred Colonel Foster's displeasure. We found him an amiable figure of fun and something of an antidote to our somewhat humourless Commanding Officer. He retired to bed, continued to smoke and eventually set himself alight, suffering fatal burns. I'm afraid his was a doubtless loud but ignominious exit from this troubled world.

During my time at Netley, my mother came to see me and said a tearful farewell. The appalling casualties of the Great War were very much in her mind, and she was convinced that she was saying goodbye to me for the last time. I couldn't help feeling that she might well be right. Fortunately, she was accompanied by my cousin Yvonne Bevan who gave us both support. It was not the happiest of partings.

These uncertain days were alleviated by regular nightly visits to the Bugle at Hamble, whither I repaired with Dick Handley to whom I shall refer later. The Bugle was a typical English pub with polished brasses, excellent beer, and a genial host. Among its later patrons was an Australian anaesthetist who was destined to serve in the siege of Tobruk. He committed a blackout offence whilst in the Bugle, inadvertently leaving his inadequately masked sidelights on. Fined for this, the demand for a small sum of money pursued him during his absence abroad, and eventually caught up with him in Tobruk many months later. He paid it and sent a polite letter of apology for the delay to court, which sent him with his receipt a charming expression of good wishes, which he framed. He told me all this when I met him in Egypt later in the war, when we worked together. I should add that the siege of Tobruk was a famous and heroic event in the history of the war, which was front-page news for many months.

The fact that the correspondence took place and came to a successful conclusion is a tribute to the Army Postal Service, which kept up high standards throughout the war, making huge contributions to the general morale.

A major feature of the scenery was the liner Queen Mary. We had an excellent view of her as she lay in Southampton Docks. At first, she sported red funnels with black tops. Her superstructure was white. Each day she became greyer, as painters worked like bees. They completed their work within two weeks, before we left for France. She became one of the main troop carriers of the war.

Chapter 3

France

Two weeks after the Declaration of War, we sailed in an ancient overcrowded cargo ship for Dieppe. The weather was rough, the ship crammed with soldiers. Seasickness was rife and it was not the most pleasant of voyages. We were an early part of the British Expeditionary Force, two divisions strong. We were billeted near Dieppe while an unsuccessful search was made for our hospital and its equipment. On the first Sunday, I attended church and listened to an appropriately belligerent sermon by an army chaplain. We belted out 'Onward Christian Soldiers' and followed it with a rousing rendering of another hymn to the tune of 'Deutschland Uber Alles' doubtless to the bewilderment of the French civilians in the road outside.

Six weeks later, we were allotted someone else's hospital outfit and were sent to a bit of farmland near Offranville, some six miles outside Dieppe. In a remarkably short space of time, the tents were erected and many of the 1,200 beds were in place.

The next eight months were those of 'the phoney war'. The winter was hard and at first it was not easy to keep warm. We had a little medical and surgical work to do, but most of the time was spent in boarding (i.e. classifying) soldiers, many of them Territorials, who had somehow escaped the medical net before disporting themselves in drill halls in the UK. We even found an amputee or two, and sent them home. There was very little fighting and we saw very few casualties. Such as there were came mostly from the region of Metz, where they had received surgical treatment in a Casualty Clearing Station from

RS Handley, my old Netley friend. He was later to grace the staff of the Middlesex Hospital, as had his father, Sampson Handley, a famous pioneer of breast surgery. After the war, Dick was to make his mark in the same field. It is difficult to think of a more charming or more delightful colleague.

At this time, I made some lasting friendships. Our medical specialist was a man of culture and great ability. At home, he had been a pioneer in the setting up of a rheumatology clinic in the Postgraduate Hospital at Hammersmith. He had studied in the Sorbonne and spoke French fluently. In World War One, he had served as a Lieutenant in the Grenadier Guards, an experience that had enabled him to understand and accept many apparently irrational aspects of military behaviour. He was like a father to me, and his quiet humour and understanding were endearing qualities. He became my guide, philosopher and friend. His name was WSC Copeman. Sadly, he was to die at a relatively early age after the war. His memory is one I shall always cherish with gratitude.

Dick Magnus was a morbid histologist, already of some fame as a research worker at Kings College Hospital. He was born a rebel. He was extremely intolerant of any form of discipline and suffered fools less than gladly. He was thin as a rake and had an enormous appetite for protein food. He made me his confidant regarding his views on the enormities committed by some of those in authority over us. His marriage was in process of breaking up at home, which in no way sweetened his outlook. Still, he was good company and I developed much affection for him, as he had a highly developed sense of the absurd, a good feature in anyone. He survived the war, only to die of a heart attack in his late forties.

Another but less congenial activity of the hospital was as a 'last chance centre' for medical officers who had let the Demon Drink get the better of them with their units. Alcoholism was a Court Martial offence. Doubtless we were chosen because of our CO's reputation as a strong disciplinarian. I cannot remember a single officer surviving his probation. On a notable occasion, a young officer arrived in a taxi during one of the Colonel's dreaded inspections. It was a soaking wet day, the ground covered with puddles. The official cortege was an impressive one. The great man was accompanied by the Hospital Registrar, Company Officer, RSM and other dignitaries. Descending from his taxi the boy, very much the worse for wear, was confronted by this awesome assembly. He gasped and fell forwards into the mud where he stayed, unable to rise. The colonel ordered his removal under arrest, and he was ignominiously carted off. His military career was a short one.

In the evenings, there were opportunities to indulge in the gastronomic delights of France, as rationing had not started in earnest and shortages were not yet apparent. The local French people were friendly and good to us. One occasion sticks in my mind. Following dinner in Le Lapin Blanc in Dieppe, half a dozen of us found ourselves without transport back to Offranville. We were told that les sapeurs-pompiers might be able to help us. At the Fire Station, they told us that they knew of only one available taxi driver, and that he was in the brothel. We had no difficulty in finding this institution or the taxi driver who was enjoying a glass of Pernod in the company of a number of mostly middle-aged ladies with gold teeth. The majority wore dresses which buttoned all the way down the front—and very little else.

There was a versatile man at the piano who also liked Pernod. We bought a round of drinks for one and all and in no time the party was in full swing. We thought the Palais Glide would be most appropriate, and so it proved. The girls were enthusiastic and apt pupils, as was the pianist. We were relieved when the taxi delivered us back to our camp in one piece.

These times provided wonderful opportunities for improving any rudimentary French we might have had, but being dyed-in-the-wool Brits, we did not take them up to advantage, and had little to do with local French people who were kind and hospitable. A delightful young French interpreter called Serge Corbin was attached to our unit. He was the son of the French Ambassador in London, spoke perfect English and was full of life and fun. One of his hobbies was vintage wine, and he and I spent some happy times exploring dusty cellars grubbing about among cobweb-festooned bottles. An occasional shout of triumph proclaimed a special find. He taught me much.

Another Frenchman to whom I became devoted was the official interpreter to the Dieppe medical base, Dr Jules Lechaux. He had been a family doctor in St Addresse, Le Havre and was married to a forthright American lady who, he said, spoke French with an execrable accent. He was a man of strong right-wing views, and a member of 'Les Cagoulards' (the 'Hooded Ones', who were strongly anti-communist and not above a little occasional terrorism). I found him to be a typical

fiercely patriotic Frenchman full of Gaelic humour and gay in the
original sense of the word. He was later to run the local Resistance in
Le Havre. He got caught and paid for his sins with a spell in Auschwitz
Concentration Camp. I managed to trace him after the war, and visited
him in his retirement home in the Midi. He was a truly lovely man and
brave as a lion.

We soon learned how to live comfortably, even when the weather
was at its coldest. Small Valor stoves were permitted in our tents. In
highly irregular fashion, I improvised in my own a small urinal that
consisted of a hosepipe with a filler end, leading to a soakaway at a
discrete distance outside. It proved a boon on icy nights, and was
admired by those whom I let into the secret. For company I bought
myself a singing canary, which boasted curious black eyebrows. He was
immediately named Neville, in honour of Mr Chamberlain who was
similarly endowed, and became a popular member of the mess.

The Company Office and the officers' quarters were situated in
an orchard, while the hospital itself was spread over adjoining fields.
We had a tented operating theatre, in which we treated a few surgical
emergencies and minor complaints.

Our immediate superior, Lt. Col. Smith, informed us that certain
irregularities had developed in a hospital in St Nazaire and that he
was being posted there in order to clear up the mess. In his place came
Lt. Col. Ogier Ward, a famed urologist and a Great War hero. In that
conflict, he had been in the Royal Horse Artillery and his exploits had
gained him a chestful of medals. We respected him very much. He was
most meticulous in everything he did, and under his aegis the Surgical
Division developed into an efficient unit though Fate was to decree that
there would be no opportunity to make use of it as intended.

I was given unexpected Christmas leave. I stocked up at the NAAFI,
and sent an official telegram giving the time of arrival of my train at
Swansea, and ending 'inform Dr Williams'. In due course, it reached
my father as 'uniform Dr Williams'. On the way home, a careless officer
dropped his valise outside the British Customs. There was a sickening
crash of broken glass and huge quantities of wine and spirits spread over
the floor. As there were strict rules regarding the amount of drink one
could import, this event did nobody any good. At home rationing had
not yet really started to bite, and there were no bad shortages except for
booze. There was a mood of completely unfounded optimism regarding

the war but this was soon to change for obvious reasons. I enjoyed a happy time amid family and friends, and returned to Offranville much refreshed.

During this time we were joined briefly by Robert Cox who had been a Registrar in Surgery at the Westminster Hospital. He was later to become one of Sir Stanford Cade's right hand men and rose to be a Consultant. After the war, he became Consultant Surgeon to the Army, and in due course was awarded a CBE. He became President of the Hospital Rugby Club at the time of a golden era in its history. Robert, like me, was a great admirer of our new OC Division, Lt. Col. Ogier Ward. This meeting marked the start of a lifelong friendship.

While at Offranville, I must confess to becoming just a touch more military in both my appearance and behaviour. The early promotion of 'specialists' to the rank of Major, had aroused a certain amount of jealousy and resentment, understandably, among regular officers who felt they had been leapfrogged - and so of course they had. We became known as 'chocolate majors' and had been given a sizeable jump in pay. For me this meant little as I had no dependants and there wasn't anything much to spend the money on anyway. A crown replaced the couple of pips on each shoulder. This promotion meant that we were elevated to the starry heights of 'Field Rank', and this brought certain privileges in its train. One was that we were permitted to wear riding breeches and boots as in theory we were mounted officers even though no horses had been available for many years. I went to a French tailor who ran me up a very smart pair, which I still possess, though they are more than a touch tight round the waist. They created quite a stir when I flaunted them in the mess. I was sorry when the next day there appeared on the notice board an order that said that unofficial dress had been observed in the mess and that such practice would cease forthwith. I did not wear them again until after demobilisation more than five years later.

I also felt that my youthful appearance would be enhanced if I grew a moustache. I cultivated a rather weedy growth on my upper lip accordingly, brushing it outwards in the guardee manner. It eventually became I thought quite impressive and in spite of some derision I managed to preserve it until the end of the war. I still have a photograph taken in 1940 that shows it well.

Field Officers were saluted by all ranks below them, so walking in the streets of the Dieppe base was a busy business. We carried 'Swagger Sticks' to keep our hands out of our pockets, but I soon substituted this for a dried bull's pizzle which an enterprising friend obtained for me. The thick end was quite weighty, so it constituted a useful defensive weapon. I did not however go to the lengths of having a silver tip made for it. We also carried gas masks in the early days, but these were soon removed from their khaki webbing cases which proved to be useful shopping bags.

Near the hospital lived a delightful couple, Eric and Elsa Douglas-Dufresne, with their two young children, Alain and Elise. They ran a farm in a quiet area. Eric was three-quarters French in ancestry, but a typical and complete English public schoolboy, whilst Elsa was three-quarters English by descent but charmingly French, both in speech and gaiety. Both were bilingual. We went many times to dinner at their home. Wonderful food and wine was followed by French songs around the piano, which Elsa played beautifully. She sang like an angel too. I still remember nearly all the words of 'Aupres de ma Blonde' and 'Parlez moi d'Amour' among others. My constant companion at these relaxing evenings was Rex Binning, my anaesthetist colleague. Rex and I had shared digs as students in London. He was most competent and had an impressive air of savoir-faire which with his quick wit endeared him to the ladies - perhaps a bit too much so, as of his four marriages, three fell apart. He was excellent at his job, suave and unflappable. I found him great company. I had managed to get my motorcycle sent over from the UK. It had a pillion and considerably widened the scope of our social life. We made frequent trips to Gruchet where Eric and Elsa held open house. One particular evening stands out in my memory. A tasty main course was followed by a remarkable sweet, prepared by their attractive maid at her own request. It consisted of a pineapple ring in which was planted half a banana, the top of which bore half a glacé cherry. A couple of grapes at the base and a generous dab of Crème Chantilly completed the picture. Rex and I bit our lips. 'I'm sorry about this,' said Eric gravely, 'but Marie-Madeleine got engaged last week.'

Back at No 3 General things weren't so good. Most of the other ranks had been Territorials who did not take too kindly to the somewhat harsh discipline imposed by Colonel Foster, our CO. He was a man who knew his drill book well but not the new kind of soldier, or indeed the new kind of officer he now had to command. His inspections became dreaded, as any minor deviation from the details he deemed important, such as the provision of an ashtray for every bed or the tension of the tent guy-ropes, was at once picked up and the young officer responsible given an irate public dressing down. There was not a great deal to do, and boredom among the men was rife. Misbehaviour was common and always heavily penalised. There arose, mostly among the other ranks, a seething discontent, which in April 1940 started to manifest itself in a somewhat unpleasant way. First the Sergeant Major's tent went up in flames. Not long after, the Company Office was reduced to ashes. Then the outlying empty wards started to catch fire. Patrols with officers in charge walked the hospital at night; nobody was ever caught. There was an atmosphere of fear and mistrust. We had to censor the men's letters home and from them the degree of disillusionment became rapidly apparent. Most of the soldiers were illiterate and unable to express their thoughts, but a few did so well. There was clearly much unhappiness and homesickness. Some showed a strong leaning towards communism. However, all this was suddenly to change—and in a big way. Little did any of us guess what the near future had in store.

On 10 May the Germans struck with almost their entire army, leaving on their Eastern Front (on the Polish border with the USSR) hardly enough soldiers to collect custom duties, according to one of their generals.

We prepared to receive large numbers of casualties, which never arrived. A hospital dance in the Sisters' Mess in the local chateau went ahead as planned and became known as 'The Eve of Waterloo Ball'. It was a somewhat apprehensive affair, not helped by the collapse of the dance floor at the height of the festivities. Doubtless it had not been subjected to such strains for a couple of centuries.

French and British fighter planes, which had run out of fuel, landed in a large field adjoining the hospital. They acted as decoys and were soon joined by others, and before long we resembled a major air base. We waited for what we thought would be an inevitable air attack, but it never came.

The news that the Germans had reached the coast to the north of us in the region of Le Treport and that lines of communication with the front had been cut was a shock. The prospect of receiving any wounded patients disappeared. Confusion reigned. We had not treated a single casualty. Surgical and anaesthetic specialists received orders to pack a single suitcase each with emergency belongings and embark in ambulances. We did so in the belief that we were going forward to work in Casualty Clearing Stations, but it soon became apparent that we were moving away from the fighting. We were indeed part of a 'save the specialists' movement. We went westwards along roads crowded with refugees. Meanwhile our hospital received orders to pack up and load onto a train. We carried out the orders so expeditiously that the enemy in due course captured the entire unit intact, except for the surgical instruments that the company officer had the foresight to cram into his pockets. He also had the presence of mind to commandeer my motorbike, which bore him westwards until it ran out of petrol and he abandoned it. I never saw it again, not surprisingly.

We were not harassed by the Luftwaffe and thankfully reached Cherbourg without mishap. There we were sent to a French Military Hospital that was full of wounded soldiers who had been through bad times. Some were 'bomb happy', and became hysterical when under attack. We were rightly told that in the event of air raids we were to stay in the wards with the patients, and not go to the shelters built in the hospital grounds. In due course, there were night raids and part of the hospital was knocked down, but without casualties. One night the shelters received a direct hit, and were largely obliterated. They were empty at the time. Fate had been kind. After a few days of uneasy existence while the Dunkirk evacuation was taking place we had orders to embark on a cross-channel packet boat. There was a little light relief at the quayside. A particularly handsome colonel had, like many of us, lost his tin trunk. Unexpectedly he spotted it and rushed to open it. Alas, all he found was a large framed photograph of himself in full dress uniform. Our boat was heavily loaded with soldiers who mounted on deck a single Bren gun doubtless as a gesture of defiance. We were told that there were Heinkel bombers looking for us, but mercifully we saw nothing hostile and were much relieved to reach Southampton intact. Some of my colleagues followed in another ship after some adventures that had left them without rations for two or three days. This was reported to Plymouth, to which port they were heading. They were disappointed to receive the reply 'Sorry no meal at present available, but marine band will attend.' It did, but it was a while before hunger could be assuaged.

On arrival, I reported to the War Office where they told me to go home and await orders.

Before doing so, I paid St Thomas' a visit, only to find the hospital very much as I had left it. Many staff had returned to work there following the evacuation in September, and patients were drifting back. The shaking events that had befallen Europe and our army seemed to have made little impact. But attitudes were shortly to change, and profoundly. The outlook then seemed to be one of uncomprehending disbelief.

Half a century later, a series of articles on wartime events was published in the St Thomas' Gazette under the title of 'Fifty Years On'. Included were some remarkable pictures of King George VI and Queen Elizabeth standing in the ruins of the bombed-out hospital. It had suffered terrible damage and some serious casualties. Among the dead was the son of the best-known forensic pathologist in the land, Sir Bernard Spilsbury. He had worked as a student on my firm. He was tall, handsome and delightful. He had been working in the basement theatre when a bomb pierced the hospital building and exploded in the next room. Thereafter the hospital moved out to Hydestile in Surrey where it stayed for the duration.

The moustache in 1940

Tented hospital in France

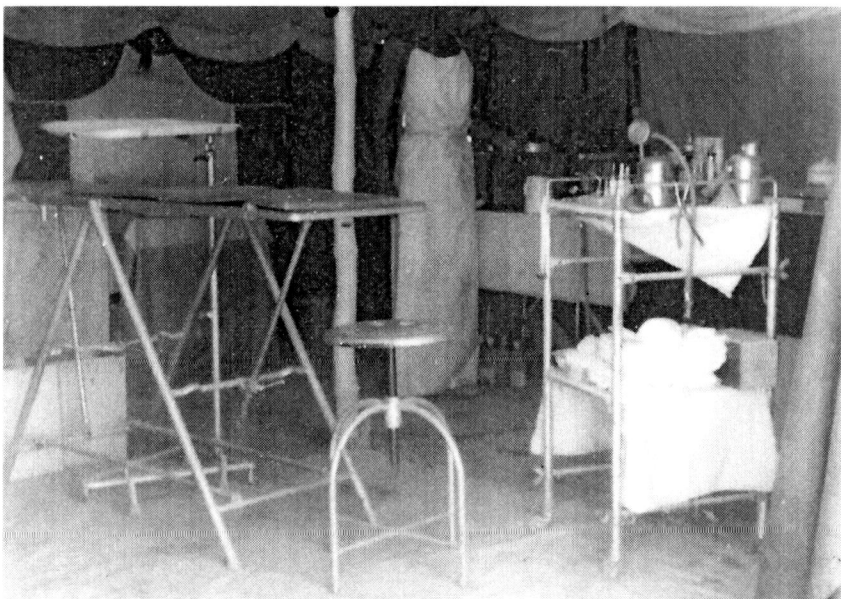

Operating theatre

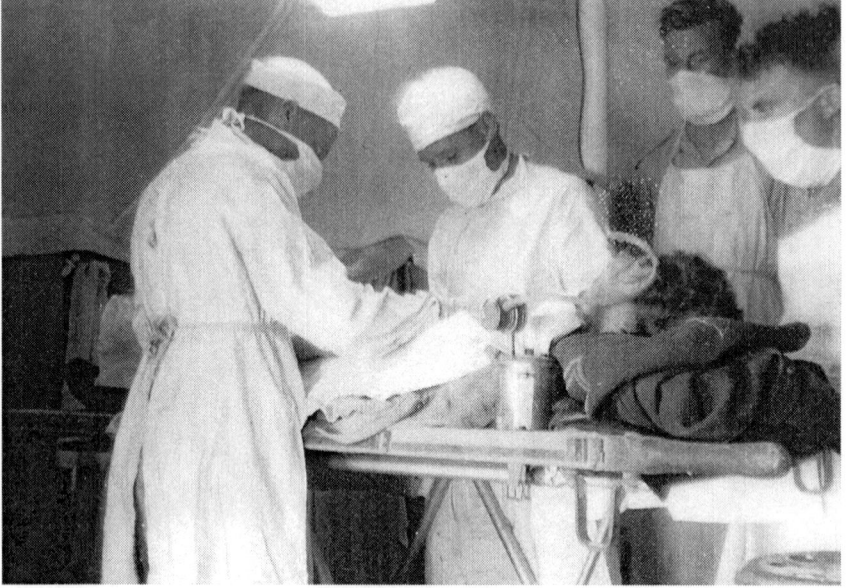

Operating theatre in use

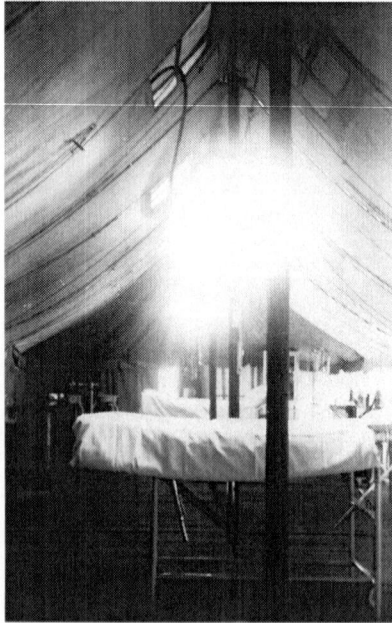

Shedding light on surgery

Chapter 4

Home, Sweet Home and Beckett's Park

My parents, who were convinced I had been lost, were much relieved to see me back. My mother and I spent a peaceful week in a small hotel in Horton, a little seaside village in Gower. There we heard Churchill's famous speech, which started 'The news from France is very bad' and finished 'We will never surrender.' It put great heart into one and all at a time of deep depression and hopelessness. Everyone was aware of the great losses we had sustained in both men and materiel and how weak our defences were; though the will to fight was strong there did not seem to be much left with which to fight. In fact, Churchill himself in his memoirs confessed that he did not know what would have happened had Hitler decided to attempt an invasion before we had had a breathing space in which to rearm.

After an all too short and anxious holiday, instructions came to report to Beckett's Park in Leeds. As I left, I remember singing with some feeling the old First World War song:

'I don't want to be a soldier; I don't want to go to war,

I wants ter 'ang arahnd Piccadilly Undergrahnd

Livin' upon the earnin's of an 'igh born lidy'... etc, etc.

A crowded train took me to Leeds where I met some old friends. We were to form the nucleus of a new hospital, No 8 General. No 3, not surprisingly, was disbanded. We were billeted in the town, and were daily harangued by regular staff on the need to salute smartly and to conform in the manner of dress. Our mentors were people who had not yet heard a shot fired in anger. During this time we saw a great deal of the inside of 'The Royal Oak', a pleasant enough pub in Headingly, of which I retain some happy memories not least of which was the quality of the beer. The local populace, like nearly all North Country people, were warm and friendly. We were issued with tropical kit, which gave rise to much speculation as to our destination. Our guesses were not helped by a colonel of artillery who said that this was the second time he had received such an issue. On the first occasion he had finished up in Norway where his stay had been very brief and uncomfortable, the whole campaign lasting only a month.

I had a message from dear Rex Binning who said he had found digs in Headingly where he was living with his wife. I went to the address he gave me and found the front door open. In I went and shouted 'Rex'. A woman's voice answered. It said, 'Come upstairs; I'm in the first room on the right. Rex is out'. It was as she said. The room was full of steam and she was luxuriating in the bath, whence she continued the conversation. I had never seen her before and felt a little out of my depth. I wisely took the first opportunity politely to withdraw. That marriage, Rex's first, did not last unduly long.

A few weeks later we entrained for Glasgow, where we embarked in the good ship Andes, and sailed towards Greenland, on 3 August 1940.

Chapter 5

Middle Eastward Bound

The SS Andes was a new ship, built for the meat and passenger trade with Argentina. Ours was her maiden voyage. Officers were six to a first class cabin intended for two, and travelled in reasonable comfort. The men were not so lucky, living in very crowded conditions in the lower decks. We sailed down the Clyde in company with two other liners, escorted by warships that soon disappeared. We were told they were just over the horizon, a tale not widely believed. We made a huge Atlantic detour, starting off in the direction of Greenland. Our first stop was two miles outside Freetown where we anchored and took on water and stores. We were not allowed ashore because of the malaria risk. Nevertheless, we contracted some six cases. Anchored nearby was the Hospital Ship Maine aboard which were some friends from St Thomas'. They asked me to dine but this too was not permitted. Thence we sailed across the tropics. The waters were phosphorescent and the flying fish marvellous to behold.

Our next stop was Cape Town, where we received a warm if wary welcome from the inhabitants. Wary because the convoy that had preceded us had carried numbers of wild and sex-starved Australian soldiers on their way to the UK. They had run riot in the black townships, and done all sorts of things that the South Africans hoped white men would not do. Our lot behaved themselves surprisingly well, and we were most hospitably entertained. My 30th birthday I celebrated in a posh country club in Muizenberg where some well meaning South African friends insisted I drink a traditional Rainbow Cocktail. This proved to be a fearsome and rather sickly multi-coloured potion that I downed amidst cheers. It was not long before I regretted so doing as I got violently drunk and sick. It was not a birthday on which I look back with undue pleasure, and have not felt partial towards liqueurs ever since. The wind blew up that night and we could not get back to our ship. The Navy came to our rescue and we spent the night aboard a county class cruiser, a very pleasant experience. The Senior Service proved itself most adaptable.

The remainder of the voyage seemed to get hotter and hotter, and we made no more landfalls. In the Red Sea, I recall watching a friend swallowing soup while the sweat poured off his chin into the bowl, and wondering if I was witnessing a sort of fluid form of perpetual motion. His name was Johnny Crofton. He was later destined to become famous as a physician in Edinburgh, and a pioneer after the war of the treatment of tuberculosis with a new drug—streptomycin. We had a destroyer escort the crew of which wore shorts only, their torsos burnt almost black. Never had I seen such a tan. As for me, I had my first experience of prickly heat. I do not want another.

At Port Tewfik, we saw the Empress of Britain, flagship of the White Star line. Little did anyone guess that she was about to depart on her last voyage. A remarkable book has been written called *To War with Whitaker*. The authoress of this spirited account was an aristocratic lady called Countess Ranfurly. She sailed in her as far as Cape Town, where she jumped ship as she wished to rejoin her newly married husband back in the Middle East. This act of indiscipline may have saved her life as the Empress was sunk by enemy action in the Atlantic with heavy loss of life on her return journey to Britain. Whitaker I may say in passing was her butler. He had joined the army and managed to keep in touch with Her Ladyship in a commendably faithful way throughout the war.

We disembarked in blazing heat on 19 September. I wondered how much more I could take. In the event, four summers were to pass before I returned to Britain. Some enthusiastic officers marched their companies from port to camp when the temperature exceeded 120°F. A few men sustained fatal heat stroke. Later such foolishness became a court martial offence.

Chapter 6

Alexandria

After a few days of roasting in a desert camp, orders were given to entrain for Alexandria, a cosmopolitan haven of civilisation where No 8 General Hospital set up shop in the Italian School in the district of Chatby. The school was large, clean and white, the walls of its main rooms embellished with the words DUCE DUCE DUCE in foot high capitals in honour of Italy's dictator. These sad symbols of a regrettable regime were soon painted out, theatres and wards equipped, and an 800 bedded hospital was in business, with medical, surgical, orthopaedic wards and a maxillo-facial unit, or Max Factor Company as it was irreverently called. My ward was run by an ex-St Thomas' sister, for whom I had great liking and respect. Her name was Helen Luker, and she lived in Petersfield. It was a joy to work with her. Alas, she contracted severe hepatitis, a common scourge in Egypt and was destined to die early after the war. Another delightful sister, an Irishwoman called Kitty McShane, ran the officers' ward. She became famous when Randolph, Winston Churchill's son, was admitted after an accident when serving with the Long Range Desert Group. He had broken his pelvis. Randolph tended to be stroppy and was not a popular character. On one occasion he brandished a letter in front of her saying 'Do you know who this is from?' He let her into the secret: 'The Prime Minister'. 'Good Heavens, from Nahas Pasha himself,' was her somewhat deflating reply. The Pasha was then PM of Egypt, and not the most loved of characters.

In those early days there was little fighting; the surgical department was largely concerned with accidental injuries and common emergencies, together with minor cases. The medical side was mostly concerned with dysentery, sandfly fever, hepatitis, malaria and a host of pyrexias of unknown origin. The workload was not heavy. The officers lived in some state in the Windsor Hotel. Leisure pursuits were well catered for in the local Sporting Clubs, which provided tennis and squash as well as good swimming pools.

Alexandria (Iskanderieh in Arabic) is a wonderful place. It is Egypt's chief seaport and second largest city. Alexander the Great founded it in 332 BC, and it was the capital of Egypt for a thousand years. Its famous lighthouse, the Pharos, was one of the seven wonders of the ancient world. Its remains have only recently been discovered by underwater archaeologists.

This idyllic existence was too good to last, and before long I found myself posted with a Surgical Team to the 2/5 Casualty Clearing Station at El Daba in the western desert half-way between Alexandria and Mersa Matruh.

Chapter 7

With the Army of the Nile

My orders were to go by train to El Daba a small Arab village, two stations beyond that of El Alamein, on the Mediterranean coast, some thirty miles from Mersa Matruh. Matruh was at the end of the railway line, not long built, for both military and touristic reasons. King Farouk of Egypt had given Matruh his personal blessing by staying there with attractive female company while his beautiful and popular Queen Farida was giving birth to his child shortly before the outbreak of war.

At Alexandria Station, I met an old friend, John Watts, who was also on his way to the 2/5 where he was the surgical specialist. John had been a house surgeon at St Thomas' a year before me, his chief being a remarkable and charismatic man called Philip Mitchiner. Philip was uninhibited and mercurial. He spoke with a cockney accent and had a very quick wit. He was a great teacher with a fund of extraordinary stories that he embellished with short Anglo-Saxon words. Philip feared no one and could not tolerate pomposity of any kind. He was also the Commandant of the Hospital Officers Training Corps. John had taken his advice and joined the regular RAMC. Tales of PM's confrontations with his colleagues and the rather prim and proper Nightingales of the nursing staff, including the very formidable Matron, Dame Alicia Lloyd-Still, were legion, and are still remembered and retailed by many. As a result he was worshipped by his students, who included John. John himself was to have a remarkable career. He had already served in Palestine where the Arabs killed a number of British soldiers who were trying to discharge the difficult duty of keeping the numbers of would-be immigrant Jews within the agreed quota allowed under the Balfour Declaration. This supported the creation of a homeland for the Jews in Palestine. Later the Jews took a hand and murdered a number of their protectors, a not wholly unfamiliar story.

John and I had an interesting journey to El Daba past airfields which contained numbers of dummy planes, the nature of which was clearly visible from the train. Daba turned out to be a small collection of flea-ridden mud huts, and was almost deserted. Halfway between it and the cool blue Med was our CCS, a cluster of tents in a dusty clearing in the desert. Our sole protection was a few slit trenches. A few miles to the west was an airfield that supported a squadron of Blenheim light bombers. Beyond them, at a place called Fuka, was a fighter base. The full moon was dreaded, as it brought an occasional air raid by Italian bombers. The tents acted as microphones and we often heard the drone of the machines from afar. The crump of the bombs made the ground bounce, but no one was hurt. We had little to do, and I was able to enjoy test flights with the RAF next door. One little story has stuck in my mind.

My pilot friend had been flinging his aircraft about the sky, doubtless with the intention of making me sick, when I reminded him that he hadn't told me what to do if we had to abandon ship. We had parachutes strapped to our backs. He pointed to its handle and said; 'When I tell you, get hold of that, and go to the back. There you will find a hole in the floor. When I say, jump through it, count to three very slowly and then pull the ripcord. In the RAF, we have a modification of this procedure—simply say 'Jesus Christ Almighty, pull.' Happily, this necessity never arose. Later the squadron were transferred to Crete where most of them were lost.

Life was reasonably smooth but the troops' language was bad. We had a much-respected padre who got fed up with it, as almost every sentence contained a four-letter word. He addressed a parade and told them that swearing was useful as a relief of feelings when one had something to swear about but highly undesirable when it just coarsened speech. He finished his harangue by saying 'Now you lot can bugger off.'

I received orders to put together a small surgical team. It had an anaesthetist and a general duties officer, a sergeant operating room attendant, and a few other ranks. We had our own sterilising equipment and a number of drums that contained dressings and drapes. Our instruments were adequate but the stocks were not lavish. After a month, we were told to report to a Field Ambulance in the sand dunes outside Mersa Matruh. Its commander was a GP from Birmingham, Lt. Col. Bekenn whom everyone liked and respected. His unit was tented but we were given a small underground hospital that the Egyptian army had previously constructed. It was built of concrete and had a thriving population of mice and fleas. There we set up shop near Cleopatra's Pool where the Queen was reputed to have swum with Mark Anthony.

It was about this time I had an interesting contact with the Royal Navy. A very splendid naval commander came to our hospital to ask if we could render service if one of his ships bringing supplies for the desert forces should be hit, a request to which I readily acceded. As he was speaking a petty officer came up, saluted smartly and handed him a message which the office scanned and said 'My compliments to Mr Smith. Tell him to use his loaf and stop farting about like a blue-arsed fly.' 'Aye Aye, Sir,' and the PO was off. I often wondered in what guise those words reached the young officer concerned. I later discovered that our colourful visitor had been a gunnery officer at the Battle of the River Plate. This Naval action, in which some German warships had scuttled themselves rather than be sunk by gunfire, had come as something of a tonic to the nation after the disastrous events of Dunkirk.

When the Italians invaded Egypt soon after Mussolini had declared war, energetic patrolling by the 7th Armoured Division (the original Desert Rats, so called after the attractive little jerboas which seemed to exist on nothing in the desert) had caused them to withdraw into fortified camps near the Libyan border. Some of our patrols had secretly penetrated some of these camps and surprisingly reported hearing women's voices. The intelligence report had concluded 'It must be borne in mind that these high pitched voices may have belonged to enemy personnel who had served in Abyssinia.' It later transpired that the Italians, mindful of the needs of their troops, had established brothels in the camps. (It was in due course, back at the base that I had to treat one of the Mesdames who had a huge ramifying fistula-in-ano. Bearing in mind the old adage that the patient after proper treatment should look as if he or she had just got away from a tiger, I operated with complete success.)

Lt. Col. Bekenn told us at dinner in the mess one night that an attack was planned for the next day. We finished the meal with a heart-felt toast to the men concerned on the morrow.

In the event most of the Italian army was taken prisoner with the minimum of losses to our own troops.

General Wavell's Army of the Nile was hardened and well trained, and well led by Generals Wilson and O'Connor. Security was good and the action on 6 December 1940 took the enemy by surprise. The first reports stated that five acres of officers and 200 acres of other ranks had been captured. Later, the figure of 113,000 personnel was given. Our own casualties were relatively light, but the lines of communication between the front and ourselves were long and many of the wounded came to us in very poor condition and too late for us to do much for them. One I recall was a well-known English international rugby forward named Rew. He had been shot through the abdomen and was mortally ill with peritonitis. I operated but it was much too late and he died. But another, named Alastair Down, who had lost an eye, survived and became, many a year later, the President of the CBI as well as the Business Man of the Year. His efforts earned him a knighthood. He was an old Marlburian, and I met him again at a meeting of the Marlburian Club in the 1970s. Another of our patients was Giles Isham, an actor whom I had seen a year before in a charming play in London called *Lady Precious Stream*. He was a survivor too. Our patients came from the Australian and Indian Army Divisions as well.

Officers were starting to develop their own distinctive style. Corduroy trousers and silken cravats were de rigueur, but the 11th Hussars (the Cherry Pickers) always wore their red trews and the Inniskillings their green ones. A general chose his ADCs from each regiment, and they became known as his port and starboard lights.

We were never close enough to the fighting to be in any danger, but a piece of foolishness nearly cost me dear. Always a keen motorcyclist I was delighted to find abandoned a motorcycle with a full tank. I went for a spin in the desert, where a lone Italian plane spotted me, and honoured me with a stick of five bombs all to myself. I lay in the shelter of my machine and the last bomb came close, covering me with stones and sand, and making my ears sing. I lay very still until the plane, doubtless thinking he had scored a direct hit, disappeared over the horizon. A short sharp dose of terror can be most salutary. It gives one an idea of what the troops at the sharp end may have to endure for days at a time.

Matruh gave me my first experience of battle surgery. We dealt with several convoys of wounded and sick officers from British, Indian and Australian units. All had had long, painful, and unpleasant journeys from the scene of battle; they were exhausted, and many were in poor condition. Clearly our unit was situated much too far from the fighting, a fact which I duly reported. These early experiences led to the formation of small mobile self-sufficient surgical teams, later called Field Surgical Units, which could set up shop with other larger mobile medical units (Field Ambulances and Casualty Clearing Stations). The service these new formations were able to give was vastly more effective and results very much better.

The fighting apart, another source of death and disaster was the discovery by the Australia Division of a large drinks depot in Bardia. Alas, they fell upon this with considerable enthusiasm. Many got hopelessly drunk and perished in the desert of exposure, the nights at that time of year being very cold.

All that now remained for the Army of the Nile was to clean up the remainder of the Italian Army, which had ceased to offer resistance. The advance continued as far as Agedabia on the Gulf of Sirte. General Wavell received orders to send some of his forces to help the Greek Army who, having put up a very good fight against the invading Italians, were now facing invasion by the well-equipped and trained German Army which had come down through the Balkans. There they had overrun without too much difficulty the slender opposition offered by the Yugoslavs. This depletion of our military strength left the desert forces dangerously weak, a fact that Rommel and his Afrika Korps were soon to exploit.

We were called back to Alexandria. My team was disbanded.

Chapter 8

Alexandria Again

I rejoined No 8 General Hospital, where the workload was still by no means heavy. I was glad of the opportunity to improve my tennis in high-class company. There were many very good players in the Sporting Club at Alex. In my own unit was Douglas Freshwater, who had represented England and was an enormously gifted player. He also possessed a keen sense of humour. Other members of the Sporting Club included a Greek Davis Cup player and others who had played in Egypt. Squash was also on the menu.

There followed a welcome period of rest and recreation which was interspersed with enough work to keep one from getting stale. At this time, we had a good liaison with the Navy, who shared a hospital (No 64) with the Army on the outskirts of the city. Also in harbour most of the time was the naval hospital ship, HMS Maine. One of her surgeons at that time was an old St Thomas' man, Bob Wolfe, whom I already knew and respected professionally. He would come over and help with problem cases, and from time to time, I would dine with him aboard his ship.

The Navy in port was not all that safe. Two Italian mini-submarines, each with a two-man crew, sneaked in and severely damaged with limpet mines two battleships, the Queen Elizabeth and the Valiant.

I remember going into the Union Club one evening for a drink. Next to me at the bar was a young naval officer whose hand was shaking so badly that his drink was spilling. He apologised saying he had just been through a bad time. That was an understatement. Not long after

I was invited to look over his ship, HMS Illustrious, by a naval gunnery officer, Ackworth, who was a relative of one of my St Thomas' friends. She had just run the gauntlet of the Luftwaffe in returning from Malta where she had been doing convoy work, and a number of heavy bombs had hit her, with much loss of life. The damage was enormous with twisted metal everywhere. The young naval lieutenant I had met had indeed been lucky to survive.

Alexandria we found to be a rich city in which the wealth was largely concentrated in the hands of a few, mostly Greek, people. Many had made their fortunes from cotton. Life for the moneyed classes was a leisurely and well-organised affair. There were two beautiful Clubs—The Sporting and Smouha—that had fine tennis and squash courts and swimming pools as well. The sun shone every day and in the winter, the temperature was equable. The shops, mostly run by Greeks, had adequate stocks of most things needed for everyday living. The middle classes seemed to have come from all over the world, but some were of Egyptian origin too. Of the latter, many were Copts who claimed to be the true descendants of the ancient Egyptians, the Arabs being interlopers who came later. The masses were Arabs and extremely poor. Food was mercifully very cheap, and the ordinary fellah could fill his belly with *Aish* (unleavened bread) and *Hommos* (beans) for three piastres of which there were 100 to the Egyptian Pound, which was of a little less value than the British one. Most Arabs were thin, but there was little evidence of malnutrition. We lived well in the mess but 'Gyppie Tummy' (diarrhoea and vomiting) was common.

The medical hazards were many. Poor hygiene was at the back of some, such as dysentery, infectious hepatitis, and polio, which claimed the life of one of my friends, Kenneth Eden, a neurosurgeon of repute. The commonest diagnosis on the medical record card, the I.1220, was PUO (pyrexia of unknown origin). There were multitudinous cases of fever for which no cause was ever discovered. I myself contracted sandfly fever, an unpleasant but common complaint said to be transmitted by the bite of a sandfly, a small hairy and ubiquitous insect. Fever was accompanied by meningism and a nasty headache. I did not enjoy the experience. Malaria was rare. I saw one case of smallpox, and very frightening it was. Most Arabs had developed immunity to the things that were the scourge of the Europeans. It was sad to note that water was unsafe to drink some fifty years later, and had to be drunk from sterilised, sealed bottles.

Following my return from my foray with the Army of the Nile, I was given local leave. This I spent with Douglas Freshwater in Mena House, a fine hotel near the Pyramids. The Great Pyramid of Cheops or Khufu is said to have been built in about 2500 BC. It was for millennia the tallest building in the world and is now the only survivor of the Seven Wonders of the Ancient World. Sadly, weather and tourism both play their parts in eroding it, the other pyramids, and the Sphinx. Its preservation will indeed be a mighty task. We enjoyed a good leave. Little did I guess that my next visit was to be on the night of my wedding.

Douglas was the hospital dermatological specialist, and also the venereologist. VD was rife in Egyptian cities, the brothels of which did a roaring trade with the troops and was responsible for much sickness. Syphilis and gonorrhoea were rampant, as was soft sore. Sometimes a soldier would contract all three together, in which case he was said to be suffering from the Unholy Trinity. One day Douglas invited me to come on a tour of Sister Street, Alexandria's Red Light District. I found it a somewhat shaking experience. We had to carry loaded revolvers and the Army and Navy went on patrol together. The area was sleazy in the extreme. In one street was a row of cages, in which women of all ages displayed their dubious charms, while would-be customers walked up and down deciding what would be their choice. Inside the buildings were scruffy rooms, each containing a bed and cupboard. HQ had become alarmed at the high incidence of disease and had ordered that each room should have a bottle of permanganate as well as washing facilities. It was obligatory for each woman to wash and douche in between each client. It was our duty to ensure that the women knew what was required of them in these respects so we had Egyptian interpreters with us. The place was full of drunken soldiers, mostly Australians, who from time to time would kick a door, and shout 'Hurry up, you bastard!'

We would wait for the customer to leave a room and then enter it. The woman would be asked to produce her bottle and sometimes she could not find it. She would then be asked what she was supposed to do. Many didn't know. Those who failed this simple examination would be arrested and taken to the Egyptian authorities, presumably for further instruction. I was later told that some women were accepting forty men a day.

The army Warrant Officer who was with us was a somewhat overbearing man who tried to teach the Petty Officer who I suspected was more experienced in these matters. The result was an unpleasant inter-service dispute, which gave rise to an official complaint from the local admiralty.

At the end of the evening I felt I had seen humanity at its lowest ebb. Douglas also took me on another occasion to 'Mary's House' which was the homely name given to the Officers' Brothel. This was, to coin a phrase, a very different kettle of fish. The ladies concerned were mostly Greek and engaged in feminine pursuits such as knitting and embroidery. Gold teeth were popular. Most were middle aged rather than young and were not (to me at least) very attractive. The main room had a piano and a well stocked bar. It all seemed very clean and civilised compared with the awfulness of what we had previously seen. Our inspection revealed nothing untoward. Later it received a direct hit from an enemy bomb that caused fatal casualties among one or two of the clients. I was informed that the authorities had a considerable problem as regards the choice of official classification that would go to the relatives. Should it be 'killed in action' or 'killed in the execution of duty'? I suspect that 'killed by enemy action' would have met the bill best.

Alexandria swarmed with pimps anxious to cater for officers' sexual needs usually by offering their sisters, or so they said. They used to hang about in the street outside the Windsor Hotel. I must confess that such temptations were not difficult to resist! Less dangerous evening entertainment was provided by open-air cinemas that had huge screens and showed a variety of American films.

We lived well in the mess, but 'Gyppie Tummy' was common. Occasionally blood heralded dysentery. We learned then to look out for appendicitis, whose symptoms dysentery could mask.

Our CO was an amiable Scot, who scanned the Army List with regularity, looking for news of promotion or death, and now and then scoring out names above his with satisfaction.

After a long delay, the post had started to come regularly. On occasions the letters had been sodden and then dried. They bore a stamp 'Salvaged from the Sea'—a reminder of the price that was being paid by those who were trying to get them to us. Mail was an enormous morale booster, but sometimes it could have the opposite effect. A wife wrote to a soldier saying she had heard that he was being unfaithful and asked what the woman concerned had that she hadn't. The answer went 'Nothing, but she's got it here!' I received an unexpected parcel that had been chasing me since my days in France. The good ladies of my mother's parish church in Morriston, my hometown, had sent it to me. It contained a hand-knitted Balaclava helmet, scarf and pullover, for which I'm afraid there was little use in Egypt.

Time passed pleasantly enough. Tennis and squash at the sporting clubs kept us fit. Work was interesting but certainly not excessive. An Egyptian doctor who had trained at Barts, one Hassan Sobhy, introduced me to tropical medicine in his local hospital. We had a few soldiers, mostly victims of accidents, to look after at our hospital. No 8 General was also the home of a Maxillofacial Centre, run by an Australian plastic surgeon named Champion, and by Eric Dalling, an oral surgeon of distinction, destined after the war to be appointed to the Royal Portsmouth Hospital where he was to found a new department which came to enjoy a great reputation.

But this comfortable life was too good to last. In the early spring, I was posted to a Cairo hospital, and left No 8 with regret.

Chapter 9

Cairo

No 63 General Hospital at Helmieh outside Cairo was situated in what were once Egyptian army barracks, with a block of new purpose-built wards with an air-conditioned operating theatre block attached to them. Luxury indeed!

In charge of the Surgical Division was a Manchester surgeon, Tiny Holt. He was a huge man with a distinguished reputation. He had a sharp mind, was helpful, but basically rather idle. His medical counterpart was by contrast a very small man who had been a physician in Hull. Lt Col Muir was a convinced communist, but did not seek to press his philosophy on others. He was, maybe surprisingly, a jolly little man. I remember him entering with gusto into a postprandial mess rag after which he went smartly into right-sided heart failure. If he survived the war, I do not think he can have lasted long. Our orthopaedic specialist was Ewen Jack, a tall good-looking Scotsman who had been in the SS Andes with us and there met a beautiful and very nubile QA nurse whom he later married in Egypt. Sadly, in the course of time, she became enamoured of a libidinous colleague of mine and the marriage to Ewen broke up, to the surprise and sadness of many. Ewen at the end of the North African Campaign was destined to take over No 6 Field Surgical Unit from me. After the war, he was appointed to the staff of the Royal Infirmary, Edinburgh, only to die of cancer of the kidney a few years later. His was a tragically short life for one so gifted.

Life for the next year was good. There was enough work to keep us interested and busy, and my colleagues were a pleasant lot. The Medical

Division was occupied, as in Alexandria, with treating a variety of fevers and tropical diseases, whereas we served the local base units and gave secondary treatment to those wounded in the series of battles with the Afrika Korps under Rommel, which raged along the North African littoral. These were largely between mobile units and swayed back and forth. In the forward areas, life was hazardous, very uncomfortable in the heat, and very tough. Those of us, who had the good fortune to be at the base, led a relatively comfortable and civilised life.

For the first half of 1942 I continued to live in safety and comfort in No 63 General Hospital. We were quartered in huts and each officer had a room to himself, with a bed, chair and a desk. The washing facilities were good. We were close to a large Mess with its own garden, frequented by hoopoes, and with a large frangipani tree the flowers of which gave off a heady scent. Food was reasonable, we had a ration of one bottle of beer a day, and for those with a taste for stronger drink there was Greek gin (Bolanachi). This was real firewater and was downed with fizzy lemonade which we called by its Arabic name of 'Gazooza'. Any overindulgence was followed by truly fierce hangovers, so drinking tended to be moderate.

The Mess was run by Tony, a local Cypriot who was proud to describe himself as a 'British bloke'. He had an amazing understanding of cats. The mess swarmed with them and he could do anything with them. He was the only human I have met who could call a cat to him by name. Later, at the time of the Suez episode, the Egyptians murdered him brutally. The mess servants were either Egyptians or Sudanese, and were called Suffragis. They were kind, loyal and reasonably honest, and gave good service.

I joined the Heliopolis Sporting Club where I regularly played tennis with Egyptian friends. They were all of a high standard. Three I remember particularly well. Hussein Allouba worked with an Egyptian civil aviation company that was the forerunner of Misr Airlines and Egyptair. He played a considerable part in the early formation and post war expansion of those companies. Shafei was an officer in the Egyptian Air Force. He had played for Egypt in the Davis Cup, and had a son who in the seventies got through several rounds at Wimbledon. The third member of our group was named Talaat, a Turk, and like Shafei had been a member of the Davis Cup team.

In the club restaurant we were on occasion joined by a bull-necked and grossly overweight young man who would sit down to a huge pile of beef sandwiches all by himself, and wash them down with soft drinks as his religion demanded. He was King Farouk, a man despised for his gluttony and womanising. He had a charming and lovely queen called Farida. Perhaps surprisingly, he did have a spark of humour, and indeed of wisdom. When asked what he thought was the future of monarchy as a world institution, he replied 'In ten years time there will be only five kings, the Kings of Spades, Hearts, Diamonds, Clubs and the King of England'.

During this period, my games playing reached standards never before or since attained. I was asked to play an Exhibition Match against the then champion of the world at squash, and later Egypt's ambassador to the UK. His name was Amr Bey, and he was a most polished gentleman. To my astonishment, against all the odds, I won the first game. Perhaps he wasn't trying too hard. I was giving my all. I managed to hit him in the mouth with my racket, following which he bled profusely. He was an immaculate figure and always played in long white trousers that now became bespattered with blood. He said nothing, but from then on, it was a different story. Another improbable event was when I entered a Cairo tennis tournament, and found myself up against the champion of Egypt in the first round. His name was Najar. I had been up late at a party the night before, and had a dreadful hangover. The first set was a disaster, and he began to fool about. Then suddenly I could do nothing wrong. I went hard for my shots and they all seemed to go in. He started cursing and was unable to pull himself together. I came through two sets to one, and there were banner headlines in the Cairo press 'Najar battu par joueur de la moyenne classe': not very complimentary but satisfying all the same.

There was quite an active social life in Cairo at this time, and there were no real shortages. Among my civilian friends were some very nice Egyptians, mostly games players, and a cosmopolitan assortment of Europeans. Among these last were Kaula and Dodie Senutovitch. Kaula was an exiled White Russian whose very aristocratic family had been wiped out by the Bolsheviks, for whom he had a passionate hatred. He had managed to make a pile of money in Egypt in the oil industry. He and his wife entertained on a lavish scale, giving parties in his fine house, usually with a White Russian balalaika band in attendance.

Dodie was English, and a gentle, sweet woman, who was always good for a laugh. At their home, I met a variety of people including American business friends. I recall talking to one of them who worried about his country's performance should the USA get involved in the war. 'I guess' said he 'that we are such a goddam hotchpotch.' His anxiety was not justified by subsequent events.

In December 1941, the Japs attacked Pearl Harbour, and the US was in with us. We had been alone for 17 months, and the issue was still in doubt. Now it was not. The news came through on the mess wireless in Helmieh. The silence that followed was broken by someone who said 'Now we will win.' And so we did, but the struggle was to be long, hard and costly.

Meanwhile we had been driven out of Greece, the army retreating to Crete with heavy losses and many warships sunk. Later, the enemy took Crete and our lot together with a number of Cretan fighters who were, as Kaula neatly put it, 'exCreted'. Many of our own soldiers and sailors were wounded and came to No 63 for treatment. We also looked after a number of Cretans. They were a fearsome bunch of literal cutthroats, who had killed many German parachutists. Most of them sported huge black moustaches, and once their wounds had healed, started wiping off old scores among themselves, and, having tasted blood in quite a big way became very difficult to control.

Finally, in June 1942, Tobruk fell and Rommel captured a large quantity of materiel and took many prisoners, mostly South Africans, who had taken over its defence from the Australians and us. The siege, one of the epics of the war, had lasted 18 months, had been once lifted only to be renewed after a brief period. The Afrika Korps swept on towards Egypt but halted at El Alamein where there was a bottleneck, 35 miles across, between the Quattara Depression and the sea. The Quattara Depression was impassable to tanks, and there was for a while an easing of hostilities. During this time, Generals Montgomery and Alexander arrived on the scene. Auchinleck was replaced. He was a fine and brave soldier and had done the best he could with limited resources. He came to see the wounded in my ward. He was a very big strong man, a typical soldier, and much admired and respected. He survived the war, eventually to retire to Birmingham where he died in his nineties.

During this interim period, there was a huge build-up of our forces for a battle that was to mark a turning point in the whole war. Monty would never go into action until he was sure that his forces were superior to those of the enemy in every way, and there was no question of failure. During this period of building up, Colonel Cameron, who was then the CO of No 63, sent me to make a report on the conditions at one of the camps in the forward areas. My driver and I reached it by way of a military road that was crowded with vehicles of all kinds. A peep through the canvas covers of some of the lorries would reveal tanks or guns inside, thus, concealed from the prying eyes of reconnaissance planes.

Soon after my return to base, I was told to put together and train a Field Surgical Unit, Middle East Pattern. One of the first half dozen to be raised, it was a mobile operating unit designed to work with a host unit, usually a Casualty Clearing Station (CCS) or a Field Ambulance (FA). The personnel were two officers (a surgeon and CO [me], and an anaesthetist). In our case, the latter was 'Daddy' Hammerton, who was a bit older than the average, and a paterfamilias. There were seven other ranks, who included a corporal operating theatre attendant, (Blackett, pleasant, willing and efficient), a clerk (Bailey, educated and reliable), two drivers and a factotum (Millen) who happily loved digging, thus later contributing to our safety and peace of mind. We had two tents to form the operating theatre and a practical but no means generous assortment of instruments and anaesthetic apparatus. We also carried a field operating-table, sterilising facilities and drums, as well as a small electrical generator to run the lights. All (men and materiel) were conveyed in a three-ton lorry and a Ford V8 staff car. Both vehicles were new and many envious eyes were cast upon the staff car by senior officers. We knew that a decisive and critical battle was imminent. It came as no surprise when in July we received orders to go forward from No 63. They came shortly after the High Command was changed and Generals Montgomery and Alexander took over. Montgomery in particular was like a fresh, reviving wind. He made radical changes at once. He was a great believer in the value of publicity and it was not long before all the Eighth Army had seen him and been addressed by their new Chief, who was here, there and everywhere.

In due course, we joined a vast procession of military traffic that moved steadily in a huge cloud of dust towards the front. Our destination was Burg el Arab, a small Arab town, not far from which we joined No 16 CCS, already a desert hardened unit. With them, we set up shop and dug ourselves in.

Field Surgical Unit at El Alamein, 1942

Setting up shop on arrival

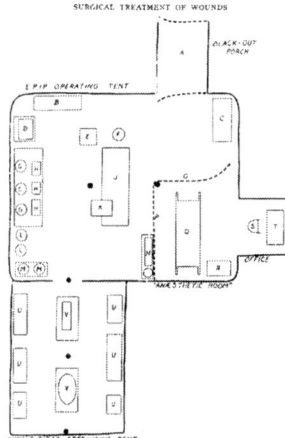

Plan of tented operating theatre as used in the battle

Major Keith Lucas sets up his blood bank

Chapter 10

El Alamein

The July heat was terrific, but our new hosts were situated within easy walking distance of the blue Mediterranean, the blessed waters of which were cool. The bathing was superb, and always in the nude. I had myself appointed official photographer to the unit, and took a number of group pictures after insisting that all the bathers adorn themselves with fig leaves picked on the way to the sea. There was no problem keeping these in position, as all that was necessary was to face the wind. On one occasion, I fell asleep on the sand. Some unknown person took this opportunity to borrow my camera and take some very personal snaps. I was not a little surprised when the prints came back from the developers.

Somewhat to our dismay, the order came through soon after we arrived that all Red Crosses were to be removed from tents, vehicles, etc for security reasons, as their presence might have given away where casualties were expected in the battle that was obviously about to be fought. At this time, we did not enjoy the air supremacy that we later gained, and we suffered sporadic attacks from dive-bombers. I recall grovelling in the dust just outside the theatre on a moonlight night with a stream of tracer bullets coming at us. They fell short; nevertheless, it was a chastening experience. The plane shot up the Quarter Master's Store, one of the bullets penetrating five tins of Elastoplast, and coming to rest in the sixth. There was sporadic enemy shelling, but we were out of range. Our side did not return fire, as the gunners were busy plotting the position of the German guns, ready to deal with them later, without giving away their own positions.

A certain chivalry existed at this time during the desert war, both sides respecting each other as soldiers who were doing their duty under conditions of great natural difficulty. Both sides listened to the haunting strains of 'Lili Marlene' on the radio, a song full of nostalgic yearning for normality and love. Later on, when news of German atrocities leaked out, this spirit tended to die, the war becoming more vengeful and brutal. The Germans did their own cause little good by persistently booby-trapping bodies in the hope of catching those who came to bury them.

No 16 Casualty Clearing Station was replaced by No 10 CCS. Its surgeon was Donald Douglas whom I found to be a charming and delightful colleague. He was an extremely competent surgeon, who had studied in the Mayo Clinic, in Rochester in the States. He was a Mayo Fellow. I could have not had a nicer or better colleague and I developed great personal affection for him. He was a marvellously good second opinion in a difficult case and gave me all possible support. (After the war, it came as no surprise when he became Professor of Surgery at St Andrews, and later President of the Royal College of Surgeons of Edinburgh). The Commanding Officer of No 10 CCS was by contrast a rather vain gentleman, known as 'Suspensory Socks', a play on his double-barrelled name. When he heard that after the expected victorious break through there was a possibility that we might meet some of the Uled Nail, that is, troops of dancing girls in the Libyan cities, he sent for his smartest uniform. Needless to say, there never was an opportunity for him to don it.

A rough outline of the medical arrangements at El Alamein was as follows. Behind the fighting formations, which had their own regimental medical officers, were the Field Ambulances, whose prime tasks were the evacuation of casualties to surgical centres, usually located in Casualty Clearing Stations where emergency surgery to render the wounded fit for travel back to base hospitals in the Nile Delta was undertaken. Alexandria was some forty miles away, and Cairo about one hundred and twenty. We also enjoyed the help of a first class blood transfusion service. The donors were soldiers at the base, who were given a pint of beer for each pint of blood they provided. The blood taken was all of the group O (Universal Donor) kind. The blood transfusion officer, Keith Lucas, was in charge of a remarkably efficient set up. During the battle, he worked in a pre-operation tent. The entrance had a large blackboard on which he listed the patients in order of readiness for operation. The system worked remarkably smoothly and well, and the throughput of casualties was fast when battles were on. Colonel Buttle, a man of humour and charisma, ran the whole blood organisation at the base. Keith Lucas was his representative in the field. We never at any stage ran short of blood for transfusion, as it was flown to several small centres together with quantities of plasma. A pleasing feature of this very special service was that occasionally one of the bottles in the blood crates turned out to be whisky.

Our host Casualty Clearing Station was one of a group which included South African, Australian, and New Zealand units with whom we worked in total harmony. It was interesting to note how much bigger on average the Commonwealth soldiers were compared with our own. Doubtless, the open-air life they led in their early years, together with a body building diet, was responsible for this. The Australians also had a small advance section concealed among sand dunes much closer to the front line.

Churchill said 'Before Alamein we never had a victory. After Alamein we never had a defeat'. This statement was not quite accurate, as in 1940 two entire Italian armies had been captured, the first in Eritrea, and the second in Egypt and Libya by the Army of the Nile under General Wavell as I have described in Chapter 7. It was there I had my first experience of forward surgery under desert conditions. Then casualties were mercifully low, as there had been early surrender after relatively little fighting. A new phase of desert warfare came into being at El Alamein. Before it, the fighting had resembled the war at sea in that it had been between mobile units (artillery, tanks, and a variety of other armoured vehicles). At El Alamein the main battle was more in the nature of a set piece in the World War One pattern, but before describing it let me recall the events leading up to it. Rommel had chased the Eighth Army back to a line running from the Mediterranean in the north near El Alamein to the Quattara Depression in the south. The Depression was impassable to tanks. The front had stabilised in early July. On 30 August, Rommel attempted to break through in the south and turn the Allied flank. The Allies had foreseen this move and he was repulsed with considerable losses at the Battle of Alam Halfa, sometimes referred to as the first Battle of El Alamein.

We were situated not far from the desert railway between the Burg el Arab and El Alamein stations, a mile or two from the sea. By far the largest medical group was in the south. The CCS was of course our parent unit and provided us with our means of subsistence. It also carried all the beds and nursing personnel. It had an electricity generator and autoclaving facilities as well. It also boasted a small x-ray machine.

On the evening of 23 October a friend, Bob Stephen, who commanded a nearby Field Ambulance, paid me a visit. He told me the battle plan. Together we walked to some high ground that provided a view of the battlefield. The moon was full up. At 9 p.m., the silence was shattered and the scene lit up by the simultaneous firing of a thousand guns. Their first targets were the enemy gun emplacements, whose position had been carefully plotted during the previous weeks. The emplacements were knocked out very quickly. A creeping barrage, a tactic from the First World War, followed. The infantry crept forward in its wake. They suffered occasional losses when one of our own shells dropped short - victims of so-called 'friendly fire'.

Before long, the casualties started to arrive, and a trickle soon became a flood. The northern sector in which we were situated bore the brunt of the fighting. The work was largely 'life and limb surgery', which meant dealing mostly with chest and abdominal injuries, amputating hopelessly damaged limbs and doing our best to save others. Most wounds were caused by shrapnel, mines and machine-gun bullets. Rifle bullet wounds were rare. Our purpose was to render the wounded fit for evacuation by ambulance to the bases in the Delta. Neurosurgical cases (i.e., wounds involving the central nervous system and major nerves) were mostly flown to a special unit in Cairo, but some were treated in a specially equipped neurosurgical bus that worked not far from us. Air ambulances were few and use could have been made of many more.

Unfortunately the available surgical resources were not as well used as they might have been. Many units were held in reserve in the south where the front was quieter, in anticipation of a breakthrough that did not come for twelve days. In the north, we were overwhelmed by the number of wounded men, and my repeated requests for help seemed to fall on deaf ears. I implored Medical Headquarters to send someone to see for himself what was happening but nobody came, except on one occasion when the Deputy Director himself arrived at a rare moment when I was snatching a little sleep on the third day, so I never had the opportunity of putting the case for medical reinforcement. The situation was made all the more galling by the knowledge that there were other Field Surgical Units idle near us, and anxious to help. When after twelve days the stream of casualties started to lessen, I recall falling into bed at 6 p.m. and waking again at the same hour next day. It was the first and only time that I had ever slept the clock round. Our little unit alone had put through 180 cases, most of them major.

I felt very strongly that our resources had not been properly used. We were utterly exhausted. The failure of the senior medical staff to keep properly in touch when the heat was on had resulted in a most lamentable failure to use the mobile resources which we knew were available. My bitterness was enormous and I wrote a letter home describing what had happened. The Base Censor picked this up and sent it to Headquarters, who took a very serious view of my action as they said that it would damage morale at home. I expected to be court-martialled, but was not. I later learned that Brigadier Ogilvie, the Consultant Surgeon, had supported my protest.

In the preliminary battle of Alam Halfa, our losses had been 110 officers and 1,640 men. Of these 984 were British, 257 Australians, 405 New Zealanders, 65 South Africans, and 39 men of the Indian Army. In the main battle of El Alamein, we lost more than 13,000 men, the ratio regarding nationalities being much the same as it was in the 'curtain raiser' battle.

War is a foul, dirty and dangerous business. Young men of all nations concerned are trained to kill, maim and hate, controlled and directed by older men further back, who are themselves in comparative safety. In a few it brings out the worst, but in many it brings out the best, and reveals hitherto unsuspected capacity for bravery and heroism. With it too comes a deep sense of lasting comradeship. I formed for our soldiers an abiding respect and admiration. Their courage and toughness will always live in my memory.

I have often been asked about my own feelings at times such as these. In the course of the battle, when the wounded are pouring in, there is no time for sentimentality; one simply has to get on with the job and do the best one can as quickly as is reasonably possible. It is in retrospect that the full hideousness of what one has seen is realised, and there comes a deep feeling of compassion for the young men whose bodies and often whose later lives were shattered in doing what they saw as their duty to their country and their friends. Emotions are heightened by recalling the stoicism and uncomplaining acceptance of the terrible situations that one saw so often. There seems no limit to human courage, or indeed to human folly. The Battle of El Alamein was for me the most intensive course I experienced throughout my time in the 'Great University of Life'. To have served there at a time which marked an early turning point of the war was in itself an enormous privilege.

Stuka dive bomber downed near us during the battle

Chapter 11

Westward Ho!

The battle and its aftermath over, we set off westwards along the dusty desert roads on a journey of well over a thousand miles, past scenes of wreckage and carnage, some bodies still unburied. We took the coast road through Matruh and Bardia to reach Tobruk where we saw the famous Virgin standing undamaged amid the ruins of the church, and tasted the brackish water. We treated a few sporadic casualties, mostly sappers who were in the vanguard clearing mines and booby-traps of which there were many. They suffered heavy losses. Our patients included a horse belonging to a Bedouin, who brought it to us with a huge ragged wound of its shoulder, caught in crossfire. We found an Australian bushwhacker who threw it. Our anaesthetist sat on its neck, having plugged its lower nostril and chloroformed it with a Schimmelbusch mask over the upper one while we excised and cleaned the wound. There was no follow-up possible, but the Arab owner was very grateful. It had been my first experience of veterinary surgery.

A little later, we were joined by a Queen Alexandra Nursing Sister, one of the first women theatre sisters to serve in the desert army, a splendid girl. There was heavy rain and we passed through a large group of Indian soldiers, all naked (and well endowed), washing in pools at the side of the road. Tactfully I drew her attention to a landmark on the opposite side, and thought we had got away with it. Not a bit of it. 'I have never seen a finer body of men,' she said.

Our next posting was to No 1 Mobile Military Hospital, a unique unit that the USA had presented to the Army in Greece in the early days of the war. It was commanded by Colonel CR Croft, an old St Thomas' Hospital man, who later wrote up its story. It had an operating theatre on wheels, which was to us the last word in sophistication and elegance. The CO had been a consultant physician in Plymouth, and was the father of a later member of the STH staff. It was a quiet time during which we met another STH man, Sidney O'Malley, a Group Captain in the RAF Medical Service, and an old friend from pre-war days. He was a colourful character whose boast it was that he came of a long line of Irish absentee landlords. When I confessed that we had little to do, he got me transferred to an Air Force Medical Reception Station in Benghazi. Soon after arrival, there was an air raid. The CO was David Wallace, a urologist of distinction. It seemed that he had no nerves. When I asked him the way to the shelters, he said 'Come with me.' He then took me to the top of a water tower from which vantage point we watched the display, with all manner of nasty bits of metal raining down from the sky while searchlights wove patterns across it to a deafening background of noise. Nothing touched us. 'Magnificent!' was his comment. I felt weak.

The wife of a Bedouin sheikh was admitted, very ill with intestinal obstruction, and much in need of an operation, which we arranged after resuscitation. As I was scrubbing up the sheikh came into the theatre, picked up my hand and kissed it, wetting it with his tears. From behind his back, he produced a live cockerel that he had been holding by its legs. He thrust it into my other hand. The bird fluttered madly feathers flying all over the theatre. That night the mess had for dinner the first fresh chicken for a long time.

We were then ordered to proceed to Tripoli. On the desert road Mussolini had caused to be erected a triumphal arch in honour of Italy's colonial achievements. Inevitably, it was known as 'Marble Arch'. We stopped to admire it. As we did so there was an explosion followed by yelling. On the ground lay two Jocks of the Highland Division, badly wounded by an 'S-Mine'. These devilish devices were Jack-in-the-Boxes, which jumped to head height and fired shrapnel in all directions. The Jocks had strayed on to a minefield. By walking in their footsteps, it was possible to retrieve them without further mishap. One survived, and I was grateful to do so too.

Tripoli was reached in January 1943. We were posted to an abandoned Italian Military Hospital. It was in a filthy state, with a

large human turd on the operating table by the way of greeting from
our enemies.

In that fine city we watched the first Victory Parade of the war, in
the shadow of the sculptures of Romulus and Remus and their maternal
wolf. Churchill and Montgomery were present. The Highland Division
had brought their kilts with them, and the skirl of the pipes brought
tears to many an eye, as did Winston's speech which ended 'Ever since
your victory at Alamein you have nightly pitched your tents a day's
march nearer home. In days to come when people ask you what you
did in the Second World War, it will be enough to say I marched with
the Eighth Army'

Before long, I was visited by the local medical Brigadier who was
known as 'Dangerous Dan Macvicar'. He said 'Williams, I want you to
get off at sparrow-fart tomorrow to join No 168 Light Field Ambulance
near Zuara.' He gave a map reference, miles from anywhere. After much
effort, we got off next morning and in due course reached our objective
in the middle of a sandstorm, after an interesting navigational exercise.
The CO, a London radiotherapist, welcomed me with 'What the hell
are you doing here?' I replied that my guess was as good as his. We
repaired to the mess tent for a gin, as the storm worsened. As soon as
our glasses were filled, the tent fell down on us. There was a struggle to
save the precious gin as a first priority and to get out as a second. The
second-in-command was Malcolm Duncan who was later to become a
GP and a good friend in Portsmouth. We both enjoyed a good laugh.
That night, not being the bravest man in the world, I set up my camp
bed in a slit trench, only later to find an asp in it. I managed to resist
the temptation to do a Cleopatra. We never discovered what Dangerous
Dan had in mind for us.

Our next posting was to Field Ambulances with the Highland (51st)
Division, known everywhere as the 'Highway Decorators' on account of
the large coloured HD signs that were their trade mark. We set up shop
not far from their HQ. A day or two later there was a thunderous roar in
the sky, and a number of American Mitchell bombers flew over us. We
cheered and waved but before long were beating it for cover as they let
go their bombs on the next-door HQ with considerable accuracy. It was
neither the first nor the last time that there had been such navigational
errors. We had a very busy time for the next couple of days.

Shortly afterwards there was another sad case of mistaken identity. As we finished an operation there was a great commotion outside and we went to have a look. A dogfight between some fighters was in progress. The under surface of the German wings was painted a light sky blue, but only one Spitfire was so coloured. To our horror, one of our own planes machine-gunned it from below. The pilot bailed out and landed near us. Shot through the thigh and femur, he was the next case on the table. We excised the wound and fixed him up in a 'Tobruk Splint' as was standard practice. Later he asked me if I had seen the incident. I confessed I had. 'It was one of our buggers that got me, wasn't it?' 'Yes'. 'Just wait till I get back to my unit!' He was typical of that special band of heroes!

The advance had been held up at the Tunisian border by an enemy gun in the mountains that overlooked Medenine airfield. Occasional shelling had made it unusable. Neighbouring Gurkhas were detailed to silence the gun. One day we were told their CO was startled to find the heads of the gun crew outside his tent. The famous kukris had done their work.

One moonlight night I took a walk. An enemy ME 110 fighter-bomber hove in sight, taking pot shots at anything that moved. Shouting a warning to a nearby soldier, I leapt into a ditch. The plane flew over an adjacent Bofors battery unaware of its presence. The gunners held their fire until the last moment and then let fly. It blew up with a huge explosion. I was very shaken. The soldier had remained standing throughout this drama. He spat. 'Serve 'im effing right,' was his comment as he walked on.

Our swansong was the battle of Mareth at the end of March, after which my anaesthetist colleague and I were ordered to return to Cairo, while 6 FSU went on to Sicily and Italy with new officers, one of whom was Ewen Jack, the Orthopaedic Specialist in No 63 GH when I first went there. We were sad to leave the boys, all of whom I remember with affection and gratitude. They had been a good and steady lot and all had got on well together. They had done a great job.

At the end of the campaign in Italy, the unit sent me some of its records, together with its painted sign. These have gone to the Wellcome Museum of Medical History, which passed the sign on to the Imperial War Museum. The sign and my desert boots were placed on show at the Portsmouth War Museum, which held a Fiftieth Anniversary

Exhibition in 1992 to commemorate the Battle of El Alamein. Also with them was the unit's operation book, which made grim reading. Proudly, they shared a glass case with some of Monty's memorabilia.

'Daddy' Hammerton and I sailed to Alexandria in the hospital ship Maine with a load of wounded, some of whom died en route and were buried at sea, in moving ceremonies. Such is war.

Yet it had not all been horror. I well recall waking one morning in late March after a period of drenching rain. There was an almost overpowering scent of flowers. The desert had become overnight a blue ocean of night-scented stocks, and its beauty was unbelievable. We had a sudden feeling that perhaps there was hope for the world after all. The comradeship of those days will live on, as will a host of wonderful memories.

Savouring the sweet smell of night scented stock
in the desert near Mareth, 1943

Chapter 12

Reflections on the Desert War

In retrospect, it is difficult to believe my luck in the matter of postings during these vital times, first with Wavell's Army of the Nile, and secondly with Montgomery's Eighth Army. Both were fortuitous in the extreme. All my experiences were with surgical teams, each of which I commanded myself and so had a measure of independence, and was able up to a point to choose the people who worked with me. In this respect, I found HQ very co-operative, and so was able to assemble a happy, efficient and loyal band of men, who got on well together.

Under the circumstances in which we had to work, to be going forward was all-important. A lesson that was learned early on was that, surgically, the best results were to be obtained where the time interval between wounding and treatment was short. It is much easier to achieve this situation in an advance than a retreat, when there is always a danger of being overrun and the difficulties in evacuating casualties to the base are far greater. In General Wavell's campaign we were too far from the fighting for a start, and when the opposition was routed, we lacked the transport and suitable equipment to enable us to move forward with the troops. This deficiency was realised early on, doubtless as a result of our experience, and that of those who succeeded us.

Once the Italians were driven out of Egypt, my little team was recalled to base. The army advanced very rapidly as far as Tripolitania, and its strength was then greatly depleted by Churchill's decision to send troops to help the Greeks who had done remarkably well in resisting the invasion of their country by the Italians. When the Germans came down through the Balkans to attack Greece and also sent the well-equipped Afrika Korps under the daring Rommel to Tripoli, everything changed; a highly mobile war ensued, very like naval battles between small ships. It was hard going and the fluidity of movement made it very difficult indeed to provide a proper service for the many casualties, and there was much risk that the medical teams and their patients would be 'put in the bag' as the saying was. During this time, the famous siege of Tobruk took place, and a whole General Hospital was stationed there, which did tremendous work. The surgical division included two of my friends, Ralph Marnham and IH Griffiths, both of whom later became members of the Travelling Surgical Club. I thus heard many tales of the happenings during that heroic chapter of British military history. Tobruk was on the coast and the Royal Navy kept it supplied. It remained for many months a thorn in the side of the Afrika Korps. Its presence may well have been a significant factor in preventing the Germans overrunning Egypt at a time when our forces were at their weakest. It was held by British and Australian soldiers in the earlier days of the siege, though the Australian Labour Government made determined attempts to have the latter withdrawn for political reasons at a critical time under the premiership of Fadden and Curtin. Churchill's pleadings fell on deaf ears. Two valuable warships were lost in trying to get them out. They were replaced eventually by South African troops. They had played a heroic part in the defence of Tobruk, and the behaviour of their government was a shabby betrayal. Finally, the town was overrun by the Afrika Korps, the advance of which was stopped at El Alamein.

I still remember vividly with pride and affection a number of people from the desert days, some of whom I have already mentioned. John Watts, already in the regular army at the outbreak of war, was one. He saw fun and excitement in everything, and was a most stimulating chap to have around. I have already said something about his time in Palestine before the war. He married his wife Joan in 1938 but very soon, they both found themselves in the Middle East, where I met him in the Army of the Nile in 1940, and both of them in Cairo in 1941, in time to deliver Joan of their son James. I was invited to do so in view of my previous obstetric experience. Happily, all went well, and I became James's godfather! John later served in Italy, and took part in the Normandy landings on D Day, and in due course in the crossing of the Rhine. World War Two over, he saw active service in Singapore and Java, and in the Korean War. All this he recorded in a fascinating book called *Surgeon at War*, which I recommend reading.

I owe a great deal to Heneage Ogilvie who was Consultant Surgeon to the Eighth Army. He was a well-known Guy's surgeon who had great facility with the pen. His monthly reports were a joy to read. He made a point of getting to know personally those whom he supervised, and keeping them in touch regarding the subsequent progress of the soldiers whom they had treated in the forward areas. He was very supportive when I got into trouble for my comments on the lack of liaison between the top brass and the grassroots at the El Alamein Battle. He was to write a delightful little book of philosophical essays entitled *No Miracles among Friends*. The inscription that he wrote on the flyleaf of my copy is one of my proudest possessions. Fate was not kind to him in his later years. First, his marriage broke up, and subsequently a series of devastating strokes destroyed him and his great intellect step-by-step. It was an infinitely sad process to witness.

Kenneth Eden, a young neurosurgeon from UCH, became a firm friend, in whose company I delighted. He and his unit continued with the Eighth Army after I left. To my distress, he was struck down by bulbar poliomyelitis in August 1943 and died after a very short illness. He was a brilliant surgeon and a great loss.

Keith Lucas, our blood transfusion officer, who was such a tower of strength at El Alamein, later took up orthopaedics, and became a consultant in Bristol. Keith was a hugely competent man with a highly developed sense of humour. His cheerful presence during the battle itself was an immense support.

Andrew Lowden, who was one of the first four to command Field Surgical Units in 1942, became Professor of Surgery at Newcastle after the war, and was greatly respected. He had a dry Scottish humour. He married Glenys, a truly lovely woman. Alas, he fell dead of a heart attack when walking on the moors of Northumberland in 1965. That year he had been the chairman of the Travelling Surgical Club at its meeting in Heidelberg. We all loved Andrew. Glenys continues to attend occasional home meetings of the TSC, adding her own special brand of gaiety to them all.

1992 saw the fiftieth anniversary of El Alamein, and Rosalind and I made the journey to the battlefield, where at the cemetery the dead were duly honoured in the presence of many Boys of the Old Brigade. We visited the German and Italian Memorials where moving ceremonies were also held. The desert had changed but little, though now numerous hotels, mostly empty, were strung along the coast. They had been built in anticipation of a tourist boom, which had not occurred. As we stood in the sandy, dusty vastness, a host of poignant memories came flooding back as we remembered friends no longer with us, and the stoicism and courage of the British soldiers of which we had seen so much so long ago.

'Age shall not weary them, nor the years condemn'.

Chapter 13

Cairo Again and the Holy Estate

On my return, I found the staff of the 63rd General Hospital at Helmieh had undergone much change. The Commanding Officer was now Colonel Reginald Lucas, known to everyone as 'Reggie'. He was a colourful and popular character. Born in New Zealand, he had qualified and practised there as a General Practitioner, and to my surprise had looked after a famous All-Black called Deans in his final illness. In 1905, the New Zealand Rugby Touring Team had swept the board in Britain until they came up against Wales, who beat them by a single try scored by a friend of my family, called Dr Teddy Morgan. There had been a controversial incident in which Deans, who also was a wing three-quarter thought he had scored but it was ruled that he had not grounded the ball, being pulled back from over the line by a Welsh forward, one Will Joseph, who was a patient of my father's, a Swansea GP like Teddy. As a boy in Wales I had been told this epic tale many times. Reggie was able to confirm that the last words uttered by Deans were 'I scored a try against Wales'. Reggie had emigrated from the land of his birth to Britain and had become a consultant surgeon in Canterbury. He had been a territorial officer and was a good soldier, a strong personality, and an admired friend.

The CO's of the Medical and Surgical Divisions had changed too. David Muir had gone and Bodley Scott had taken his place, a distinguished physician who was on the staff of Barts, no less. Michael Boyd, who had been the first assistant to the Surgical Unit at that hospital, now ran the Surgical Division. The two were good friends but could hardly have been more different. Bodley was a model of accuracy in his speech and work, while Michael was anything but. Bodley's outlook on life was serious, while with Michael it was a laugh a minute. Bodley never made a loose statement, while everything that Michael said had to be taken with a large pinch of salt. Nevertheless, the latter was by nature an innovator and very much a man of ideas. To work with him was for me pure joy, though most of what I learned I had to assess very carefully. I am afraid much of it proved to be simply wrong. But it had been great fun listening. After the war, Bodley rose to starry heights and deserved his knighthood. Michael, a legendary figure largely because of his eccentricities, became Professor of Surgery in Manchester (with strong support from Heneage Ogilvie) and died relatively early. He was a warm and generous man, but was in truth rather lonely and vulnerable. He was to become a godfather to our first-born son Tim. I did in fact ask him to be Best Man when I married. This he refused as he told me in the past he had been Best Man at no fewer than nine weddings and every marriage in due course had broken up.

The nature of the work was changing as the Eighth Army moved further away. The flow of battle casualties became fewer when Sicily was invaded. They stopped altogether, when the Eighth Army landed in Italy, where new base units were established. The Middle East Base HQ was still a large one and there was plenty of work to keep everyone busy.

By the time I arrived, John Charnley and Brian Thomas had taken over the Orthopaedic Unit from Ewen Jack, who had been posted to my beloved No 6 Field Surgical Unit. Ewen took the unit through Sicily and the campaign in Italy.

John and Brian were a remarkable pair. John was an original thinker who had the gift of being able to strip any surgical problem down to its basics, after which he built up a logical solution for it. He had little use for much traditional teaching. I often asked him for help with my patients and was never disappointed. He had the appearance of a mischievous cherub in those days. It came as no surprise in later years when he became the great pioneer of replacement surgery for the hip joint. This brought him international fame and in due course a knighthood. Professor William Waugh who at one time occupied the Chair of Orthopaedics at Nottingham University has written a biography, *The Man and the Hip*, in which he splendidly described Charnley's life and work. I was privileged to be able to help him in writing the section concerning John's military life in the two years he served in the Middle East as I had come to know him so well.

Brian was immensely practical and inventive, and with John had managed to obtain the services of one of the Royal Engineers' Army Workshops, which constructed to their design a multitude of pieces of apparatus for the treatment of fractures, and other orthopaedic conditions. Their combined results were outstandingly good. I well remember a tour of inspection made by the consultant orthopaedic surgeon to the Army, Sir Reginald Watson Jones, who was clearly fascinated by what he saw. At the end of it, he paid them a great compliment. He said in effect, 'It is quite ridiculous for me to have only one day in which to inspect a show like this. I would still be learning new things after a month'.

Brian's career and mine had been very similar. His father, Frank, was an ophthalmologist of distinction, as was his father before him, having founded the Eye Department in Swansea Hospital, the first in Wales. Frank was much respected both professionally and as a golfer. He had gone to Caius College, Cambridge, and it was doubtless because of this connection that Brian and I both went there. We had more or less grown up together. Brian was born in Swansea the day before me. In the early days, our family lives had merged remarkably. The Frank Thomas ménage lived in Sketty Road, Swansea. Theirs was a large, well-built house called Maes-yr-Haf. The children, two girls and two boys, were musical and formed their own dance band. Young Swansea society danced to their tunes! My brother and I spent much of our time at their house and very happy days they were. It was through Brian that I met Rosalind Bone, who was working in his ward as a physiotherapist.

During my previous stint at No 63, I had bought a dilapidated Wolsey Hornet sports car from my old friend John Watts, when he was posted away. It was in working order, but only just, and had to be treated with caution. Spares were all but unobtainable. It was a real old boneshaker, but its possession I suspect made me more popular than I would otherwise have been. When I was posted to the desert, I loaned the car to a friend who made good use of it and returned it to me still just mobile when I came back. Rosalind's friends wanted to organise a desert picnic and they asked her to obtain the use of my car. Things did not go quite to plan however as I heard that the picnic was intended to involve the use of bicycles, so when I received my invitation, I joined in not realising that I had only been asked because I was the owner of the car. The picnic was a great success and everyone was on two wheels not four. However, that was the beginning of it all! Further progress was made and Rosalind offered to darn my socks. Friendship ripened. The Officers' Mess had a nice garden, with the frangipani tree to which I have previously alluded. Under its heady fragrance one evening in May, I proposed marriage and was accepted. Tradition and simple good manners demanded that I obtain the approval of the bride-to-be's father, who was a widower. He was a retired bank manager. My letter to him, requesting the hand of his daughter, confessed that I was without any capital at all. I was therefore much relieved when he wrote back giving the green light.

Soon after, two further events that were to affect my future in important ways occurred. An Edinburgh psychiatrist, Alexander Kennedy, called to see me. During a lull in the Desert War, my FSU had volunteered en bloc for parachute training. Kennedy came straight to the point and asked if I was still keen. I explained that I had just become engaged and that my enthusiasm had waned. He immediately produced a blue pencil and scored out my name. A little later Brigadier Ogilvie got in touch with me saying that he had another surgeon to whom he wished to give experience of forward surgery and asked if I would mind if he took my place in charge of the new FSU that I was training up, in addition to my ordinary hospital duties. I did not. My place was taken by Anthony Till, always known as Tim, with whom I had been at school and greatly liked and admired. Before very long, he and his new unit were sent with a military expedition, commanded by an RAF officer, to take the island of Cos. Security had been poor, and the enemy were waiting for them. Before long, they were all in the bag, Tim Till and all. He remained a prisoner of war for the rest of the conflict. The CO was inevitably known as the Wizard of Cos, but any magical powers that he might have possessed proved unavailing.

So I stayed on in No 63, and on 14 August, Rosalind and I were married in the Garrison chapel, a structure made of corrugated iron. The ceremony was conducted at a temperature of 120 degrees by the Church of England padre, the Rev Yorke Barber, who was known as 'By Jove' by one and all. He was a charismatic character who had raced motorcycles in the Isle of Man. In the UK, he had joined the Airborne Forces, and, he claimed, become famous by scoring a direct hit on the roof of Salisbury Cathedral with a bag of vomit when doing glider training on the anniversary of his ordination. The service over, he put the wrong date on the Marriage Certificate, a mistake which was to cause some embarrassment years later. Afterwards a reception was held in the mess. It developed into a dance that continued into the small hours of the morning. The honeymoon suite had been booked in the Mena House Hotel in the shadow of the Pyramids. It was not a great success. The bed was a huge one, two double mattresses having been placed together, and the whole thing covered by a big mosquito net. Smitten by a severe attack of 'Gyppie Tummy', Rosalind had many precipitate visits to the loo. Unhappily, a stream of mosquitoes found their way between the mattresses and became trapped inside the net. Neither of us had much sleep, and had to return next day to the ward of the hospital where Rosalind worked. She was greeted with cries of 'Have you found him out already?'.

We made up for this bad beginning by having two more honeymoons, each tremendous in its own way. The first we spent in the Holy Land. After a week in Jerusalem the Golden, at that time reasonably well blessed with milk and honey, we hitchhiked to the Lebanon in two RASC trucks. Rosalind's lorry carried a load of torpedoes, while mine bore the warheads. In due course, we reached Beirut and had a blissful couple of weeks in an army hostel in the cool mountains of the Antilebanon. The second week we spent as guests of the Royal Engineers in Mersa Matruh. They were engaged in blowing up dumps of German ammunition, and were delighted to invite a gracious lady to do the honours by lighting the fuse. Few successful marriages can have got off to a more explosive beginning!

My other memory of this very special occasion is sharing a deep trench latrine with a real live general. Generals, their red lapels bearing a line of gold, were awesome figures. I felt somewhat embarrassed when one sat himself down next to me waving a flywhisk. He concluded his duties rather noisily and said 'Damn good things, these.' Loos are great levellers. Montgomery records that he and an American general laid the early plans for the invasion of Sicily in such an environment. I enjoyed my session and had no difficulty in making polite conversation with my companion, whom I found charming.

We were extremely lucky regarding our early married life. Thanks to the good offices of Colonel Reggie Lucas, we were able to live together.

There were no married quarters. Somehow, we found a flat in the slightly dingy Cairo suburb of Zeitoun, not far from the hospital. It belonged to an elegant Kuwaiti prince who we found to be friendly and nice. The rent was modest, and the facilities all we really needed. We had a living room, a dining room, a bedroom, a shower and a lavatory. The flat was one of several in a quite large building, which had a main door, guarded by a formidable looking Egyptian boab, who sat by it apparently all day, doing nothing. We had too our own suffragi (servant), called Hannafi, who kept the place clean, and did all the cooking and shopping too. He was able to get the necessities of life more cheaply than we could, while presumably securing a reasonable percentage for himself. Should we want a chicken for dinner, he would bring a live bird for inspection before cooking it. He was clean and honest, and we became fond of him. We were able to entertain without difficulty. Friends and colleagues dined with us, and now and again a visiting consultant. The great Philip Mitchiner honoured us with a visit, wearing voluminous baggy shorts and large black boots with their tabs sticking out behind. (My mother had told me as a small boy that this was not acceptable in polite society!) He was in good form, and told a ribald tale or two in his inimitable cockney. He was kind, droll and much loved by all who knew him. We also entertained Victor Dix, a contrasting character. He was on the staff of the London Hospital, a dedicated urologist, and a gentle scholarly man.

We supplemented the shower room with a bath, the plug of which discharged its contents on to the floor. Fortunately, it never overflowed into the living quarters. The summer, the last we were to spend in Egypt, was appallingly hot. On return from hospital, it was our custom to stand under the cold shower after which we didn't towel ourselves, allowing evaporation to cool us; it was the only way we could adjust our temperatures to a comfortable level. Windows were all left open at night to admit cool air and shut in the morning to trap it.

At this time, I found an obliging friend in the Royal Air Force who flew Beau fighters. I always enjoyed flips and persuaded him to take me up. As we took off from the airport, I saw the wreckage of a similar plane below us. I asked him about it. He replied 'that is what happened to the last silly bugger who tried to do what you are doing.' We enjoyed a wonderfully scenic trip over Cairo.

It was in this romantic environment that Tim, our eldest, was conceived. In due course came the joyous news that we were to be repatriated, as the Mediterranean reopened following the chasing of the enemy out of North Africa and Sicily. The operation was known as Python, and was on a first in, first out, basis, which meant I was given a place on an early ship. (Python was not to be confused with the mythical Lollipop, which stood for Lots of Local Leave In Lieu Of Python.) Rosalind's dates were a little early for her to join me aboard, so an obliging MO was kind enough to perjure himself so that the necessary adjustment could be made.

Bernard and Rosalind, Cairo, 1943

Chapter 14

Back to Britain

In August 1944 we boarded a troopship in Alexandria and made an unmolested voyage to Liverpool. We shared a table with a very godly Lieutenant Colonel and a Wren Officer who hailed from the Scilly Islands. She regaled us constantly with stories of her exploits on the sea in small boats before the war. In the Bay of Biscay we ran into some rough weather, which almost emptied the dining saloon, except for the Wren, Rosalind and myself. We stuck it out rather well, and it was with some satisfaction that we saw our naval companion clap her hand over her mouth and beat it for the heads. After that, there were no more stories of adventures on the high seas in little boats.

In Liverpool, we piloted a large quantity of luggage through the Customs without incident or search. My dear friends Tiny and Darloo Chiesman had lived in Cheshire for the latter part of the war, Tiny having become the Chief Medical Officer to ICI, a job in which he achieved considerable distinction. Charlotte, the youngest of their three children, was my goddaughter, and I had kept up with them by post throughout the conflict. We spent our first night back in the UK with them.

Tiny was a huge man with a dry sense of humour. A few words about him and his family would not be out of place. When I arrived in St Thomas' in 1932 he was a physician on the Medical Unit. He had married Darloo, a Sicilian orphan whose parents had perished in an eruption of Mount Etna and who had been adopted and brought up in the New Forest in the country home of an unmarried and well-do-do lady, called Belle. Darloo was a great beauty, with an intelligence to match. Tiny had not been able to support his family on his hospital pay and so went into general practice in Kensington, where he became an instant success. It was there that I met them when a student at St Thomas'. They befriended me and theirs became a second home. I loved them all. Rosalind and I could not have been given a warmer welcome back to the old country.

In due course, we boarded a train in Liverpool for Swansea where my parents met us. They thought, rightly, that Rosalind was the tops. A very happy leave was spent in my family home, Pentrepoeth House, Morriston, which had fortunately escaped damage in the heavy bombing that nearby Swansea had suffered in the Blitz of 1941, when the centre of the town had been almost totally destroyed. The main attack on Swansea had taken place on three consecutive nights. On the first two high explosive bombs were used, which did great damage not only to buildings but also to the water system, which included a number of temporary reservoirs. On the third night, incendiary bombs had a devastating effect. One of them had penetrated the roof of my uncle's home a few hundred yards from the central area. Fortunately, a pail of water and a stirrup pump were to hand and the fire was put out before it took hold.

After three weeks of gentle relaxation, I was posted to a small military hospital some 40 miles from my home. Situated in the heart of the Brecon Beacons, between Brecon and Abergavenny, Buckland House was a fine Victorian mansion, bought from a patrician family a few years before the war by a member of the famous Kemsley family, sons of a Merthyr Tydfil auctioneer. Lord Buckland of Bwlch was a coal owner of repute who had dominated the industry in Wales for some years. He was a powerful and feared figure, given to country pursuits. Shortly before the outbreak of war, his horse bolted and carried him under an electricity pylon, striking his head. As Dr Cresswell, his much respected doctor crisply put it: 'I received an emergency call only to find the best brains in Wales all over the grass'. Another coal magnate, Mr Llewellyn, then bought the house. It was commandeered by the War Office and converted into a hospital that served the South Wales Borderers, whose Headquarters were in Brecon and the Army Training Area in the Beacons. When I arrived, it was not very busy as most of the army was fighting with the British Liberation Army in France.

Our patients came from local army depots, while the training grounds provided a few casualties, many from Sten gun accidents. The Sten gun was said to have killed and wounded many more British soldiers than enemy ones. It was a cheap and nasty weapon carried by all RASC drivers in the cabs of their lorries. From time to time one would jump from its holder and spray the neighbourhood with lead.

My stay was a quiet one, and I certainly never suffered from overwork. The Commanding Officer when I arrived was a certain Lt. Col. Denver, a typical member of the coterie of Southern Irish RAMC doctors who constituted so large a pre-war proportion of the Corps. He was a nice kindly man with whom I used to go shooting rabbits for the Mess pot. He was as Irish as they come, and an earnest Roman Catholic. If asked by a member of the unit for leave to attend a Church of England or chapel service, he would always grant it saying 'It won't do you any good, you know'. It was through him that I met Mrs Aileen Sparrow of whom more later.

In due course Lt. Col. Mackie took his place, having, like me, previously done a stint in the Middle East. Mackie was a dyed-in-the-wool Scotsman, who had worked in the Highlands & Islands Medical Service. He walked the grounds with a blackthorn thumb-stick, proudly wearing his kilt and Tam-O'Shanter. He made it a rule not to use an English word where a Scottish one would do. This sometimes led to confusion. One of my patients was an Italian POW, whom he once asked when on his rounds, 'Do the wee oolies keep ye awake i' the nicht?' and was surprised to draw a blank response. The hospital had a black cat that soon discovered that patients' beds were warm and welcoming. The Colonel took an instant dislike to it, and if he saw it on his rounds hurled his swagger stick at it, crying 'Och I hate that damn cat; it's aye pussin', 'n squirtin' roond the hoose'.

Two months after my arrival at Buckland House, Tim was born in Swansea. The labour was quick and normal, and he was a beautiful baby. Rosalind before long brought him to stay with Mrs Sparrow, a most wonderful old lady who lived across the valley from the hospital. We showed him to the Colonel. 'Och, what a bonnie wee wain!' was his comment.

Mrs Sparrow rapidly became a close friend. She was an elderly lady with a keen appreciation and understanding of people. Her rather profligate husband died just before the war leaving her almost penniless.

They had lived in a style that he could not afford, and he had spent almost his entire fortune on field sports and high living. In order to keep her head above water, she sold the mansion where they had lived, but retained the fishing rights on the neighbouring river Usk. She had bought herself a couple of adjoining cottages that she had knocked into one. She took in paying guests, nearly all rod and line fishermen. Prominent among her clientele were the actor Michael Hordern, and his wife Eve. After the war, we went to stay with her on many occasions and sometimes at the same time as Michael and Eve, whom we came to know well. They were tremendous company.

My chief buddy at Bwlch was Kinnear Wilson, the red headed son of a most distinguished neurologist, who has a disease named after him (hepatolenticular degeneration, said to be a disturbance of copper metabolism). My friend was himself a dedicated researcher and seemed set to follow in his father's footsteps. Sadly, he was to die prematurely in the post-war years. He was a lovely colleague, full of fun and zest for life.

When at Bwlch, I received a somewhat puzzling invitation. It was to deliver a lecture at the Postgraduate Medical School in Hammersmith on the treatment in the field of gas gangrene. Throughout my adventures with the Army of the Nile and with the Eighth Army, I had not seen a single case. The desert was on the whole a sterile place. I therefore spent time with textbooks and put something together. The Dean welcomed me and we enjoyed lunch with the great Professor Grey Turner, a fearless surgeon and innovator, respected by all. He was a small eccentric man who called for tea and put his bowler hat over the pot. I discovered that I was the wrong Bernard Williams. It was my old chief that they were after! I hope my hosts were not too disappointed at my performance, which of course was really rather bogus and not the result of experience.

During my stay in Buckland House, the war started on its final phase. (We were in Cairo when the D-Day invasion by the British Liberation Army and the American Forces was announced on 6 June. We heard the news on the radio in the Sister's Office in my ward in Helmieh.) The landing seemed to have achieved almost complete surprise, but once the Reichswehr had moved their main forces to Normandy there was heavy fighting and the advance of the Allied Forces was halted with Montgomery holding the hinge of the line at Caen. It was not until late July that the Americans broke through to the south and started to swing round, trapping an entire enemy army near

Falaise. The British and Canadians advanced to the south, and closed the ring. In late August, eight German divisions were annihilated, and a rapid advance began which was to continue until there was a temporary hold-up in the Ardennes. There, amid controversy, Montgomery took over temporary command of all the Allied Armies and checked the Germans with a counter attack. Early 1945 saw the end of the last German offensive of the war. The Allies crossed the Rhine in early March. The war was as good as won.

Chapter 15

With the British Liberation Army

In March, I received a posting to join the British Liberation Army, BLA. I armed myself with a fishing rod and set forth, crossing the channel in a troopship from Dover to Ostend. There I billeted for a short while with Reginald Murley, whose company I much enjoyed. He was a forthright character with strong right wing views on most things. After the war, he was appointed to the staff of the Royal Northern Hospital in London where he soon made a name for himself. In due course, he got on to the Council of the Royal College of Surgeons, where he was elected President, doubtless because of his political abilities. He got the better of Barbara Castle in television debates when she, at the height of her career as Minister of Health in Harold Wilson's socialist government, was doing her best to abolish private medical practice!

My first job was that of surgical specialist to a hospital near Bedburg, not far from the Rhine, which had just been crossed near Wesel and Xanten by Canadian troops. The beds were filled with their wounded. Bedbug, as the hospital was inevitably called, was an austere brick building which had once housed geriatrics, a class of society for which the Germans had little use, and therefore in their thorough way had disposed of them, leaving an empty building for the advancing BLA to take over. The patients had received primary surgery from Canadian surgeons. Many had been seriously wounded, and there was quite a high mortality and morbidity among them. Bedburg was in a pine forest that was full of nightingales, which sang their hearts out at night.

A Canadian Surgeon had stayed behind to help when his colleagues had moved on with the advancing army. He was a jolly fellow with a fund of stories. He told me that he had examined a soldier who was suffering from bowel trouble using a sigmoidoscope, a tubular instrument with its own illumination. Afterwards he told his patient that he was habitually constipated, regularly dosed himself with cascara, suffered from bleeding, and came from Saskatoon. The instrument would have provided the answer to all the findings except the last, so I asked him how he knew. He replied that there was a small fragment of the Saskatoon Herald in the region.

My stay was enlivened by the arrival of a Field Surgical Unit, the officers of which I had met in the Western Desert. Fred Hannah, later to become a consultant surgeon in Weymouth, was a laugh a minute. His anaesthetist, Jake Bain, was a cousin of Eric Linklater, a famous, and somewhat bawdy, Scottish novelist. They had come across, and liberated, as the saying goes, a store of the products of Messrs Lucas Bols, which the Germans had looted from Holland. This led to many jolly evenings spent in their excellent company.

After six weeks, I had the glad news that I was to be given command of another Field Surgical Unit, with a good old friend from Middle East days as anaesthetist. John Taylor had been on the staff of the London Hospital before joining the army, and I could not have wished for a better colleague. The unit was larger than the Middle East Pattern one had been, boasting two extra other ranks. Equipment was basically the same except for tentage. A three-ton lorry and a Jeep carried the lot. Soon we set off, crossing the Rhine by way of a Bailey bridge (a structure supported by pontoons and erected in a very short space of time by the Sappers). We had become part of the final triumphal sweep of the BLA into the heart of Germany, now beaten and devastated. We had little work to do as resistance was crumbling everywhere; should any appear it was soon dealt with by the RAF, if the Royal Artillery hadn't already wiped it out.

We found ourselves attached to a Casualty Clearing Station in what had been an SS Officers' Mess in a commandeered mansion some 30 km south of Hamburg, on the edge of the Luneburg Heath. This was the time when the horror of the concentration camps was being revealed. Their existence had been known for a long time but only now did their true nature see the light of day.

It has been rightly said that the first casualty of war is the truth. As the war years went by we had become increasingly sceptical about the news we heard from either side. Behind all propaganda, there might be a grain of truth but with the passage of time, that grain tended to shrink. This is not surprising when one considers that Goebbels, Germany's Minister of Information, announced that the way to get the biggest of lies believed was to say it often enough and loud enough. Personally, I had come to take all we heard about concentration camps with a large pinch of salt, but when I saw the reality for myself, it was clear that in this case at least the opposite was true and what we had been told was really a tepid understatement. Our first official duty was to visit Belsen, a concentration-extermination camp that British troops had liberated shortly before. As they approached, they saw through the wire that its inmates were wasted and starving, some lying about too weak to move. Seeing the conditions in the camp and acting on generous impulse, they had thrown their rations over the wire and into the compound. This had resulted in a sharp increase in the mortality rate among the inmates as prolonged starvation had atrophied the lining of their alimentary tracts. This had rendered them unable to cope with the sudden glut of food that came their way. Intractable diarrhoea resulted, which for many proved fatal. Typhus and all kinds of enteric fever were rampant, as was tuberculosis.

We were kitted out with gas-protection suits and DDT powder was blown up our trouser legs and our sleeves. Barrack huts designed to house a hundred men were crammed with up to a thousand people, many stricken and dying, and lying in tiered bunks in their own excrement. Some had struggled to the primitive trench latrines, and fallen into them, perishing in their own ordure. The only ones in good nutrition were the young females who had found favour with the guards. Wasting was such that in many cases the anus was visible when the man or woman was standing. All were in striped prison uniform, some with a large J or P on their backs to indicate if they were Jewish or Polish. Each inmate had a prison number tattooed on the forearm. Circling inside the camp was a string of lorries, going from hut to hut to pick up bodies and take them to mass graves, of which the larger ones accepted 5,000 bodies, the smaller 2,000. As each layer of bodies was completed, bulldozers covered it with earth and quick lime.

In a very short time, an astonishingly efficient salvage system had been devised, in the form of a 'human laundry'. German women from nearby villages and towns had been brought to work in a series of marquees joined end to end. In the first, all body hair was shaved off; in the second, all were scrubbed with soap and warm water, using soft brushes. Then all were dusted with DDT and wrapped in clean blankets. 'Dirty lorries' brought the inmates to the first tent, while 'clean lorries' took the treated ones to the camp hospital for grading and treatment. This procedure was said to have a 25% mortality, but there is little doubt that it saved many lives overall. Numbers of medical students from British hospitals were doing gallant work under these dangerous conditions. They had their own morbidity from infectious disease. It was good to see that their number included a squad from my old hospital of St Thomas' in London.

As the army overran the compound, the electricity supply had been cut off. There was an immediate problem regarding what to do with the camp commandant, who was captured early on. Josef Kramer was a great bull of a man and a member of the hated SS Schutzstaffel, one of the most unpleasant of the Nazi organisations. Someone had the bright idea of putting him in the camp refrigerator. It was not realised that the Sappers were at work restoring the current. It was a very cold and unhappy Beast of Belsen that was eventually released. Kramer and his female deputy, Ilsa Koch, were in due course executed. Isla became even more infamous when it was discovered that the lampshades in her quarters were made of human skin.

The size of the mountain of shoe leather found in the camp was an indication of what had happened. At one time bodies had been disposed of by burning in large ovens. The ovens were common to all camps. For a long time they had been unable to deal with the number of corpses. Huge graves were then dug. Clearly the ovens had not been used for several months, as they had become rusty.

It became official policy to give as much publicity as possible to these terrible crimes against humanity. Representative sections from units of the Army were therefore required to tour the camps, as it was rightly felt that seeing was believing. Following Belsen, we visited Sandbostel, a much smaller camp but clearly one that had served the same purpose as Belsen. It had its own great pile of shoes and its quota of disused ovens and mass graves.

I found an old St Thomas' friend in charge of the medical arrangements there. His name was Ronald Murray. He and I had shared a flat before the war and we had played rugby football for the hospital. He had got his cap for Scotland and been a Cambridge Blue. He took us on a tour of the camp together with the German medical officer who had been in post when it was overrun. In the course of our tour, we had come across a body in a deep trench latrine, amidst other sickening sights. Our tour over, Ronald turned to the German and said to him 'I hope you feel ashamed of what your disgusting nation has done.'

The next camp that we visited was Neuengamme, which the advancing army had found deserted. It had however another telltale mountain of shoes and disused cremation ovens. The Germans had become aware of the worldwide publicity that had attended the discovery of the first concentration camps. In order to destroy further evidence they hurriedly evacuated what other camps they could before the Allied Armies overran them. Neuengamme itself had had a particularly bad name among camps, as it was known that large numbers of dissidents had been liquidated there. The evacuation had been very hurried and though the camp had been emptied by the time our troops got there, there had not been time to destroy the evidence of previous happenings.

During the time that we were stationed with the Casualty Clearing Station south of Hamburg, the news of the surrender of the German Armed Forces to General Montgomery on 3 May came through. This took place on the Luneberg Heath not far from where we were stationed. The news was received with great rejoicing and was appropriately celebrated in champagne. This commodity had been discovered in large quantities in the cellars of the house commandeered by our CCS, and which had previously been used as a Nazi party headquarters. During the celebrations, I acquired one of my very few wartime injuries in the form of a black eye from a champagne cork.

We had further cause for celebration when we heard that Himmler, the famous and widely hated head of the Nazi security forces, the Gestapo, had been captured not far from us together with William Joyce, an English traitor who had collaborated with the German propaganda machine throughout the war. He was an educated man who earned himself the nickname of Lord Haw-Haw. In due course he was executed, while Himmler avoided a similar fate by committing suicide by means of a capsule of cyanide, which he had managed to conceal in his mouth while being searched when caught.

John Taylor and I had the opportunity to visit Hamburg where the devastation was beyond belief. We reached it after a journey through war torn countryside full of dead cattle, their bloated bodies blown up with gas, doubtless because there were no owners to bury them. We walked along the shores of the Alster. It appeared that no building had escaped damage after being on the receiving end of a thousand bomber raids. Earlier these enormous fleets of aircraft had passed over us, the ground shaking under the roar of their engines. In the city, there was almost no sign of life. It thus came as a great surprise to hear the sounds of the Llanelli rugby song 'Sospan Fach'. They were coming from the cellar of a ruined house that the Welsh division had commandeered and turned into an impromptu nightclub complete with band. We went in and a memorable evening ensued.

Chapter 16

With the British Army of the Rhine

Not long after the German surrender the BLA changed its name, becoming the British Army of the Rhine (BAOR), the chief function of which was to restore order and create conditions in which the rebuilding of shattered Germany could start. Our FSU was broken up. John Taylor and I got posted to a small Schleswig-Holstein town called Geesthacht on the River Elbe, ten miles west of Lauenburg and near the river end of the Elbe-Travemunde Canal, a large waterway which ran north to the Baltic Sea near Lubeck. The canal marked the boundary between the Red Army and our own. At that time, the main problem was the control of huge numbers of German nationals who were fleeing westwards from the Russians, who were engaged in ruthless pillaging and appeared to have little respect for human life. Many refugees attempted to swim the Elbe and many drowned. Searchlights were trained on the river at night and a fleet of small boats was at the ready. We were instructed to set up, assisted by a small German medical unit, a basic medical service for the numerous Displaced Person (DP) camps in the neighbourhood. This was an area where there were many arms factories that had used slave labour imported from neighbouring countries. The majority of these people were Polish or Russian nationals. There were also many men and women from the Baltic States (Latvia, Lithuania and Estonia). This task was an immense one as the Poles and Russians in particular proved to be rough, undisciplined and poorly educated. Their camps were dirty and badly run. The Baltic people seemed in comparison very much more civilised. They had managed to preserve their national identity and had kept hidden not only a quantity of musical instruments but also their national dress. In spite of universal shortage of the amenities of life, their camps were clean and they had preserved some semblance of civilised living. Their countries had suffered occupation by both the Germans and the Russians. The contrast between these two oppressions had been very marked. Under the Germans, any form of sedition or dissent would be ruthlessly dealt with but suspects would be given the semblance of a fair trial; if found guilty the penalties would be harsh and included death by shooting. Under the Russian regime there was little question of a judicial process, the suspects simply disappearing and not being heard of again. I got to know some of the Latvians fairly well as many of them spoke good English. They told me that of the two regimes under which their countries had suffered the Germans had been preferable.

A German unit allocated to help us was commanded by a handsome senior German medical officer, Colonel Stein. He turned out to be an educated humane man of competence and charm. When we first met, he extended his hand to shake mine. I was not able to reciprocate this gesture, as it would have been against our orders, the official policy being one of 'non fraternisation'. I explained to him what the situation was. His reply was 'You are only doing your duty; I understand'. As things developed, we got on very well.

In our charge was a group of primitive hutted hospitals that provided care not only for DPs but also for the German soldiers, many of them severely wounded. The surgical care that they had received was very basic, and infection was rife. Bunks were arranged in tiers and sometimes pus dripped from the higher ones to the lower. Discipline among the soldiers was often remarkable. I recall seeing prone double amputees slapping their stumps together when called to attention. With the help of Colonel Stein, who spoke excellent English, a hospital service of a sort was soon established and some kind of order replaced a dreadful lack of it.

The DPs, especially the Poles and Russians, proved a very wild bunch. They raided local farms, stole animals and assaulted any farmers who tried to prevent them. In this process of establishing law and order, we had the cooperation of Russian patrols that proved to be by our standards very ruthless. On one occasion an indignant German farmer who had suffered from the depredations of lawless DPs, would not stop talking when his complaints were being investigated. The

Russian officer warned him to be quiet; when he continued to protest, the officer drew his pistol and shot him through the right hand. There was no more protest.

Special problems arose when the DPs discovered that the fuel used for V2 rockets had a pleasingly intoxicating effect when imbibed. A series of parties ensued which carried both a mortality and morbidity in the form of blindness. We did our best to get the message across regarding these dangers, but not always with success. The most receptive people were, as expected, the Balts, the least, the Poles and Russians.

I have one especially happy memory of these chaotic times. The Latvians invited John Taylor and me to their 'Ligua' (pronounced 'leegwa') festival. This turned out to be a traditional celebration of midsummer. All celebrants, including ourselves, wore on their heads huge wreaths of fresh green leaves. Their cherished musical instruments were produced, and an excellent orchestra came swiftly into being. Lovely folk songs were sung with gusto and special food washed down with beer that had been carefully hoarded for the occasion. In view of what these proud people had endured in recent years with such dignity and patience, we found it all very moving indeed.

At last, the time for repatriation arrived, to the intense joy of the Balts. The reaction of the Russians was very different. Some made determined efforts to swim the Elbe in the opposite direction. A fleet of lorries arrived, each with a huge portrait of Stalin framed in an arch of greenery. They were soon filled with Russians, the men with grim faces and many of the women in tears. We heard that this was because on return to the Motherland all were tried by a tribunal that decided whether or not they had given voluntary assistance to the Germans. A verdict of guilty was followed by immediate execution.

Chapter 17

A Fleeting Visit to Holland

Following the repatriation of DPs described in the last chapter, I received orders to join a British Military Hospital in the Ruhr. For the journey, I was allotted a pick-up truck and driver. This presented a heaven sent opportunity.

I had come to know Holland quite well in pre-war days. In 1934, I had been a member of a St Thomas' Hospital student group that had visited Amsterdam on a sort of goodwill mission; it was partly academic, partly sporting and partly social. The party comprised a dozen or so students and included members of the hospital tennis team. Our programme included a match against the Amsterdam Medical School. Much of the organisation at the Dutch end had been in the hands of Kits van Waveren, at that time on the junior staff of the Department of Medicine. Kits had been educated at Bedales School, spoke perfect English and was a great anglophile. He laughed at the same sort of things as we did. The visit proved a great academic and sporting success. For me it marked the start of a life-long friendship, Kits coming on several occasions to stay at my home, and I in turn at his in Leiden where his father was a family doctor. Both his parents were fluent English speakers. He was a great patriot and became a medical officer in the Dutch Army cavalry when outbreak of the Second World War threatened. When the German Army overran Holland in May 1940, he was captured near the border. His Army High Command surrendered after three days. He conceived a great hatred for the invaders of his country and in due course became the head of the Amsterdam Medical

Resistance Organisation, which was to prove one of the most effective of its kind in Europe. His consulting room became a headquarters of the Resistance of which he had been an active member from its early days. It was an ideal location as the frequent comings and goings were not likely to arouse suspicion. It was never raided. Kits himself had on many occasions risked his own life in working for the Resistance. A radio transmitter was concealed in his consulting rooms and a stream of messages were sent to London, giving information as to the location of arms factories and other appropriate targets for the RAF. After the airborne attack on Arnhem, he armed himself with a bottle of blood, and a Red Cross brassard. Thus equipped, he visited the British wounded soldiers in a hospital in nearby Apeldoorn. The unsuspecting German guards had let him through and he was able to obtain messages from the patients to relay back to Britain. The War Office was thus able to inform families that their sons were alive and being looked after.

Holland had suffered dreadful privations in the war, and until its liberation by the Canadians in 1945, had been on the brink of starvation. Throughout the last winter of the war, the populace had great difficulty in keeping warm and the inhabitants of Amsterdam had taken to digging up the wooden blocks that paved many of the city's streets in order to use them as fuel.

When news of my new posting came through, I had written to Kits and told him to expect a visit before long, and invited him to send me a list of food items, clothing, footwear, etc which he needed. He did so by return of post.

I found my driver to be a most cooperative chap, and planned a circuitous route via Amsterdam for our journey to the Ruhr. A well-stocked NAAFI in Germany provided nearly all the items on my shopping list. Our journey to Amsterdam was completed without any inconvenient official questions being asked at the Dutch frontier or at Army Petrol Depots. The driver and I stayed for a couple of days with Kits and delivered the ordered goods without difficulty, though one of the packets of cocoa had burst and filled the new boots with its contents. I was given a taste of the tulip bulb soup, which had helped to keep people alive during the worst time of shortage. It was not exactly palatable. The warmth of our welcome had been overwhelming, and it was not without sadness that we resumed our interrupted journey to the Ruhr.

Holland had not been shattered by fighting in the way that had befallen Germany, as much of the country had not lain in the direct path of the Allied advance. Any destruction was largely confined to the southern areas. German bombing had destroyed much of Rotterdam in the early days of the war. During the Allied advance, bitter fighting was involved in the taking of the island of Walcheren, which held a commanding position in the mouth of the Scheldt, the waterway that led to Antwerp in north Belgium as well as to southern Holland. Later, unhappily the Germans had flooded much good agricultural land in the north to create a barrier against tanks. Most Dutch people felt that this was an act of wanton malice rather than of military necessity at that stage of the war. The Netherlands had largely been bypassed by the Allies, cutting off the country complete with its German Army of Occupation. The German troops put up no resistance when the final liberation came.

For the early part of their occupation, the Germans had behaved discreetly and quietly, hoping that their presence might win some acceptance. However, behind the scenes they were busy cataloguing those who might be their friends and those who were likely to be their enemies. In particular, they listed the Jews. They put it about that Jews would be treated in the same way as everyone else if they registered with the authorities, and hinted that they would be discriminated against if they did not. This deceived large numbers of them, so the Germans had in their possession a readymade directory of names and addresses. Many Jews however did not fall for this and went into hiding, as did Anne Frank's family. Her story told the world so much, and her home has been preserved as one of Amsterdam's historical monuments.

When the Nazis turned the screw and gave orders that the Dutch doctors should categorise young men (presumably, so that they could be drafted into military service or used as slave labour) the Medical Resistance came into its own. The resignations of the entire profession arrived in no time on the desk of the local Fuhrer, Seyss Inquart. Nevertheless, there was a great purge of Jews and the intelligentsia, and many Dutch patriots found themselves in concentration camps. The Germans left a legacy of hatred and distrust that will last for generations.

Chapter 18

The Ruhr

Our destination was a large hospital near the town of Iserlohn, some 30-40 miles from the Dutch border and 10 miles to the southeast of Dortmund. Towards the end of our journey, we saw a British soldier fishing in a lake at the roadside. We stopped to ask him the way. I also inquired what bait he was using. He replied in broad Lancashire, 'They call it hereabouts Kartoffelen but I call it common or garden spud.' We felt we were a step nearer home.

Soon after arrival at the hospital, I got quite severe dysentery, passing a quantity of blood. The very enthusiastic hospital physician treated me with large doses of sulphonamide and I started to feel very toxic and ill. I asked him to reduce the dose. He refused so I discharged myself and at once got better.

The orthopaedic surgeon was a remarkable man who had been captured by the Germans at Dunkirk in 1940. When he and a friend heard that they, together with a batch of other prisoners, were to be transferred to Germany they dug a hole under the stove of their prisoner-of-war hut, filled themselves with morphia to dampen functions down, and lay doggo. Their friends replaced the stove over them. The Germans missed, searched but never found them. His friend was caught but by a stroke of luck, he got into the hands of the French Resistance, who conveyed him through France and across the Pyrenees into Spain. After the war was over, he wrote a best seller about his adventures. It makes wonderful reading. His name was Philip Newman, always known as Pip. He was awarded the DSO as a result of these efforts. I found him a fascinating companion and colleague. He had a strong suspicion that the secrets of the atom had been solved. His previous posting had been in Antwerp and a bigger bang than usual in an air raid caused him to mount his bicycle and ride off to investigate the extent of the destruction, and seek evidence of nuclear fission. It was not long before the Allies proved his theories to be correct, but in Japan rather than in Europe.

Work was light. Not far away was the Mohne Dam of 'Dambusters' fame. This was a very popular post-war film. It was about the heroic bursting of the dam across the Mohne See by the RAF. A well-planned operation resulted in the flooding of the Ruhr with dislocation of its industry. Sixteen Lancaster bombers equipped with special 'bouncing bombs' invented by Barnes Wallis were involved in the raid. The bombs were released at a low level and bounced along the surface of the water, exploding against and breaching the dam. Half the bombers were lost in the operation. The leader of the raid, Wing Commander Guy Gibson, stayed to the end and was awarded the VC. I visited the dam and found that repair had been efficient and complete.

The Ruhr is a tributary of the Rhine and its valley has been for long the main site of the German iron and steel industry. It received throughout the war a major degree of attention from the RAF and allied Air Forces. The destruction of its factories was enormous.

My stay in Iserlohn was brief and the surgical work progressively lessened as demobilisation proceeded. Brigadier Arthur Porritt, the Army Consultant-Surgeon visited us, and said that he was going to give me command of the surgical division of a military hospital in Bruges. This was an unexpected surprise. This post carried with it promotion to the rank of Lieutenant Colonel. The hospital was not open so it did not seem likely that the work would be unduly arduous, nor did it prove to be so.

Chapter 19

Bruges

And so, back to Belgium. Bruges is an ancient and beautiful city that was once capital of Flanders, and a prosperous member of the Hanseatic League in the Middle Ages. In the city centre, there is a magnificent carillon that had been silent during the war but now rang out joyously. The city's mediaeval character had been very well preserved over the centuries. It was a peaceful place in which to await discharge from the army, and to ponder the future.

In the surgical division, we made a start by setting up a sort of mini postgraduate education centre with seminars and talks on various aspects of surgery. Members were encouraged to make offerings on any subject that particularly interested them. This venture was a success.

There was at that time in practice in Bruges a distinguished elderly professor of surgery, named Jan Sieberechts, with whom I got in touch. He generously invited us to attend his clinics and operating sessions. He proved to be a forthright and enthusiastic teacher. As a surgeon, he was quick and bold. He was a great devotee of spinal anaesthesia under which he did the majority of his abdominal operations. On one occasion, I remember him doing a major abdominal bowel resection when the patient, a woman, became very restless and noisy. Suddenly all movement ceased and there was silence. 'Ah!' said the professor, 'C'est a syncope, c'est bien; maintenant nous pouvons travailler.' He got on rapidly and the patient survived, none the worse for the incident, which I may say had frightened us.

On another occasion, he demonstrated his method of removing the thyroid gland. A conscious patient was wheeled in sitting upright in a chair. After a short preamble, he picked up a scalpel and with a flourish cut her throat right across not having informed us that she had been previously infiltrated with local anaesthetic. He then divided the isthmus of the gland between clamps and removed each lobe working laterally from the centre. The operation was concluded in a very short time. Then he showed us a patient of whom he was particularly proud. Serving as a private in the Women's Army Corps of the Belgian Army the patient had been an outstanding success in many fields of sport, setting up a number of records in athletics. It had been discovered rather late in the day that 'she' was really a 'he', though the configuration of the genitalia had made sexual differentiation difficult. The Professor had set about converting the so-called woman into a man in easy stages. Clearly, he was making a good job of it, as the results so far were impressive. There was only one stage left to go. Dr Sieberechts was a man full of ideas, and brought to his surgery a considerable sense of drama, which was not lost on us.

For the duration of our stay, we were comfortably housed in a city hotel. A popular inhabitant of the house was an omnivorous parrot, which devoured with great gusto anything that was offered it including newspapers. Unhappily, someone saw fit to present it with a British Medical Journal. This proved too much for it and the poor bird died after a gallant attempt to ingest it all.

Trips to Brussels were made and friends were visited, including the parents of Philip Bauwens, a physical medicine consultant on the staff at St Thomas', whom I had known well. They were very uneasy regarding the social stability at that time. I was able to increase their sense of security by presenting them with a small Beretta automatic pistol that had come my way during the German disarmament. They were immensely grateful.

I also paid a respectful visit to Brussels' oldest citizen, Mannekin Pis. He has been living up to his name in an obscure corner for several centuries. When the British Second Army liberated him, one of its first actions was to present him with a bespoke army uniform complete of course with fly buttons, so there was no question of interrupting his ancient stream. He seemed very proud of his new clothes, as well he might be, and became very much an object of pilgrimage.

It was now August 1945, and demobilisation was gathering momentum. It was conducted on a 'first in, first out' basis, which was only fair. At last the longed for orders came through and once more, I found myself in Ostend, this time awaiting ship to take me home in company with a large number of army personnel who had been in from the beginning. Available for celebration was a considerable quantity of Guinness, but little else. In due course, I must sadly record, I felt rather nauseated. One can always have too much of a good thing.

I feel I cannot let you leave 21 Army Group on your return to civil life without a message of thanks and farewell. Together we have carried through one of the most successful campaigns in history, and it has been our good fortune to be members of this great team. God Bless you and God speed.

B. L. Montgomery

**FIELD MARSHAL
COMMANDER IN CHIEF**

BAOR: 1945

*Field Marshal Montgomery's note of thanks
when it was all over*

Chapter 20

Goodbye to All That

We had not long to wait. Soon I was once more in Ostend, and embarked in a troopship that was one of a convoy. But the joyous euphoria was marred by tragedy. In mid-channel, we received the signal 'man overboard' from the vessel in front of us, and hove-to. A lifeboat was swiftly launched. A cry went up, 'There he is!' Sure enough, a body in uniform, face down in the water came floating past us quite fast. There were feverish lunges with boathooks but they all missed, and the soldier disappeared not to be seen again. Years later, there was an unbelievable coincidence. I did a domiciliary visit in Southsea. The patient was one of an elderly couple. On the mantelpiece was the photograph of a young soldier. I asked them about him. They said he was their son who had been lost overboard from the troopship bringing him home after serving with the British Army in Europe. The date of his loss coincided with what I had seen. I said nothing.

The demobilisation centre, which I had to attend, was at Shorncliffe. There we were kitted out with the basics with which to resume civilian life. I was given a ready-made suit together with an assortment of shirts, socks and shoes. The place was plastered with exhortations to hand in all weapons with reminders that failure to do so was a court martial offence. I dutifully handed in with regret a German Luger automatic pistol which worked very well and which I had acquired during the advance, together with the rather cumbersome British revolver that all officers carried. In the case of the RAMC, the rules were that it was to be used only in defence of patients, a circumstance that was unlikely to arise. Departure from the centre was down a long corridor which was festooned with dire warnings regarding penalties which failure to hand in weapons would incur. The last notice of all was typically British: it read, 'If you have still got your weapon, you bloody well deserve to keep it!'

The issue of gents' natty suiting did not mark the limit of a grateful nation's gratitude towards its sons who had served in the forces. I was given a munificent tip of six hundred pounds with which to start to build a new life in civvy street, in addition to a row of glittering medals awarded for just being there, and a letter of thanks from King George VI, no less, and another from Field Marshal Bernard Montgomery.

And so I returned from my wanderings and was happily reunited with my family, in my parents' home, Pentrepoeth House, near Swansea. It was wonderful to see what progress our first-born, Tim, had made in my absence. Now an adventurous crawler, he delighted in filling electricity sockets with matchsticks.

Through most of the war, I had sported what I thought to be a very military moustache, carefully trained outwards in guardee fashion. It had from time to time been the object of some derision and was the butt of a joke or two during a welcome home dinner. I slipped away between courses on some pretext and quickly shaved it off. On return, I was mortified when nobody noticed it had gone.

Demob leave over, St Thomas' welcomed me back as a registrar in general surgery to its temporary wartime country home at Hydestile, near Godalming. It proved an excellent platform off which to jump into the new world that had opened up before us all. The early autumn of 1946 saw my wife Rosalind, our first two children, Tim and John, and me, living what was at first a somewhat peripatetic existence in Portsmouth. However, that is the start of another, and longer, story.

Chapter 21

Epilogue

To pass this way at all as a conscious human being is in itself a vast privilege. To do so in the twentieth century with all its upheavals and its tremendous social and historical change, as well as its enormous and accelerating technological progress, make it many times more so.

I was born in 1910 and thus have lived through two world wars. In addition, after retirement from the National Health Service, I worked as a surgeon in what was my first visit to Rhodesia. By my second visit, it had changed its name to Zimbabwe Rhodesia, by my third and fourth it was Zimbabwe. On each occasion, I worked as a senior lecturer in the Godfrey Huggins' School of Medicine. I can thus claim to have seen not only some of the horrors of World War Two, but those of an African Civil War at first hand. I was too young to remember much of the First World War, but I can recall seeing newspapers with pages covered with pictures of the fallen, and with news of ships sunk in the Atlantic with heavy loss of life. Deep in my memory too is an awareness of family distress at the loss of my father's youngest brother, who was blown to bits in the trenches in France in 1917. Neither will I forget the depths of sorrow when Rosalind's younger brother met a heroic death in Italy in 1945. He was awarded a posthumous DSO. My only brother, having survived a hazardous war in destroyers as a naval medical officer, was tragically killed in a road accident on his demob leave. He was a happy man, newly married to a lovely wife, Kate, and a full and useful life as a family doctor in Banbury would have been his. Grief at his loss, widely shared, scarred my parents' last years. These experiences left me with a great hatred of violence. I am thus very selective in my choice of programmes on the television, which so often tends to glorify it.

War is a very dicey business at best. It used to be said in the First World War that if a shell had your name on it, that was that and there was nothing that could be done about it. This proved to be the case with my Uncle Bryn and Rosalind's brother Gordon. As Omar Khayyam says 'The moving finger writes, and, having writ, moves on; nor all thy piety nor wit shall lure it back to cancel half a line, nor all thy tears wash out a word of it.'

But I was one of the lucky ones and, for me good fortune always seemed to prevail. Not only did I come through the war virtually unscathed, it also provided me with a wealth of remarkable experience and adventure, and, towards the end, with a wife with whom to live happily ever after and raise a wonderful family. It gave me too an immense respect for my country and its people for the way they faced life when the going was hard. War is often a foul, dirty and dangerous business, but it is my belief that few countries in the world can match the ordinary British Serviceman when it comes to courage and endurance when the chips are down. Amidst so much awfulness, the good stood out and was there for all to see.

I have tried not to dwell unduly on the many horrors I saw at close quarters; it was in the medical units that one saw the true reality of war, and the price that so many paid, so often without complaint.

St Thomas' Hospital Gazette, as I have already said, has published a series of wartime reminiscences entitled *Fifty Years On*. It started in 1989, and as each year passed, I made a contribution, using the material on which I have drawn in the writing of this book. The final instalment appeared in the summer issue of 1995. It was followed by a poem by Mary Leonard, which I found moving and from which I quote as it makes a fitting finish:

In Remembrance

Golden rays are the ocean still as night,
The glassy sea empty, stark as war was won,
Fireball, majestic suspended in time and space
Flames the skies over those dead fifty years ago.
Comrades joined in arms with planes, wheeling and
Reeling in the smoke-screened skies
These sands and shells too feeble to support those tanks,
Pregnant with death rumbling along those Hell-bound shores.
The sun, now solemnly destined on its course,
Rains beams on white memorials
And like a ghost supreme
Witnesses those who fell on those midnight shores.
In this hallowed hour,
We will never forget them.
Theirs is the inheritance of immortal sleep
Theirs the prize of winged victory.
We pray for lasting peace forever on this soil,
For souls of those who died for us
For freedom in this land.

Bernard and Rosalind, Llansadwrn,
West Wales, April 1992

Celebrating the Golden Anniversary,
Oxwich, Gower, August 1993

Lightning Source UK Ltd.
Milton Keynes UK
UKOW02n1546070816

280146UK00001B/10/P